Global English

Everyday Conversational English
with Airline Service Talk

글로벌 영어 항공 서비스 토크가 있는 일상 영어 회화

Welcome to
Global English!

Global English is designed for all English second language learners who are looking to improve their English communication skills. Although this book can be used by all students, *Global English* is an ideal book for students who are learning English to work in the airline service industry. It contains 12 units, and each unit is divided into interesting everyday topics to help students understand the key vocabulary, grammar structures, and key expressions related to each theme. This book also contains a section that includes essential expressions that are used by airline service employees in various situations. Every unit introduces warm-up activities, authentic conversations, comprehension check exercises, key expressions, and various practice activities related to each topic presented in the unit. Some of the units also include special reading sections to help students improve their reading skills while providing opportunities for further class discussion.

The main goal of *Global English* is to force students to use English to express their thoughts, ideas, and experiences as meaningful as possible. The intent of the book is not to have students memorize grammar rules or English expressions, but to have students understand a variety of contexts and how different expressions can be used in each context. *Global English* will provide many opportunities for students to practice and to communicate in the target language meaningfully and appropriately.

Enjoy the ride!

Contents

Scope and Sequence

Unit	Topic	Unit Goals	Grammar Focus
1	Greetings	Use informal and formal greetings	The Correct forms of the Verb Be
2	Introducing yourself and others	Understand a variety of situations and use appropriate expressions to introduce yourself and others	Simple Present-Affirmative and Negative Statements
3	Starting and keeping a conversation	Use conversational techniques to start and to keep a conversation	Yes/No Questions and Wh-Questions
4	Talking about habits and routines	Use simple present tense to talk about general facts or conditions about ourselves	Adverbs of Frequency
5	Describing people	Use appropriate expressions to describe people	Adjectives
6	Talking about vacation	Talk about vacations using appropriate expressions	Agreeing and Disagreeing
7	Expressing opinions, likes, and dislikes	Use common English phrases to agree, to disagree, and to give your personal likes and dislikes	Simple Present

Unit	Topic	Unit Goals	Grammar Focus
8	Expressing preferences	Express preferences using various phrases	Relative Pronouns
9	Providing suggestions and recommendations	Ask for and give Advice	Modal Verbs
10	Talking about past events	Use simple past to talk about past events	Simple Past
11	Talking about personal experiences	Use present perfect to talk about personal experiences	Present Perfect
12	Talking about future events	Use 'will + base verb' or 'be going to + base verb' to talk about future events	Future Tense

Global English:
Everyday Conversational English with Airline Service Talk

Unit
01

Greetings

인사말

Greetings
인사말

 Introduction

In English, greetings are used to say hello to people you meet. Depending on situations, there are different ways to greet people. When we meet friends or close family members, it is more appropriate to use informal greetings. When meeting people we do not know or colleagues in business related situations, it is important to use formal greetings. Let's learn informal and formal greetings in various situations.

Photo by rawpixel on Unsplash

Warm Up Activity

Differentiate formal and informal greetings.

Write <u>formal</u> or <u>informal</u> after each greeting.

<u>informal / formal</u>

1. Hello. How are you?

_____

2. Hi, _____. What's up?

_____

3. Good morning/afternoon/evening.

_____

4. How do you do? Pleased to meet you.

_____

5. Hi. Nice to meet you.

_____

Comprehension Check Exercise

Match the responses in column B with the greetings in column A.

<u>Column A</u>

____ 1. Hi, Jack.

____ 2. Good morning, sir.

____ 3. How do you do?

____ 4. How are you?

____ 5. Hello, Mr. Clark.

<u>Column B</u>

A. How do you do?

B. Hey, Jane.

C. I'm well, thank you. And you?

D. Good day, madam.

E. How are you, Ms. Lois?

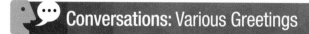 **Conversations: Various Greetings**

A. Practicing informal greeting

Kay: Hi, Tom. How is it going?

Tom: Hey, Kay. What have you been up to?

Kay: Nothing much. I am on my way to the library.

Tom: Me too. Let's go together.

B. Practicing formal greeting

Jack: Hello, professor Smith. I am happy to meet you.

Professor Smith: Hi, Jack. Welcome to my class. It is my pleasure to meet you.

C. Practicing formal greeting

Mr. Ford: Professor Lee, I'd like to introduce you to Mr. Sanders. Mr. Sanders, this is professor Lee.

Professor Lee: How do you do, Mr. Sanders? It is nice to meet you.

Mr. Sanders: How do you do? My pleasure meeting you, professor Lee.

D. Greeting passengers at the airport check-in counter

*G.S.: Good morning/Good afternoon/Good evening, thank you for waiting. Where are you going today?

**PAX: Hello, we are going to Canada.

G.S.: How many are traveling today?

PAX: Two of us.

*G.S.: Ground Staff   **PAX: Passenger   ***F.A.: Flight Attendant

E. Greeting passengers at the gate

***F.A.: Welcome aboard, sir. May I see your boarding pass, please?

PAX: Here you go.

F.A.: Thank you. Please proceed the other aisle.

 Pointers to Remember

1. The question - 'How do you do' - is used in a very formal situation, and it is used only once when meeting someone for the first time. The question is not normally used when meeting customers in service work. However, it can be used when being interviewed for a job in various formal interview settings. The question does not need to be answered. The standard response is to repeat the question again. In addition, the question - "What's up?" - doesn't necessary need a response. If you do respond, simple phrases such as "not much" or "all going well" are generally used.

2. When meeting someone for the first time, it is always a good idea to use phrases such as "Nice meeting you", "It is my pleasure meeting you", or "I am happy to meet you." When you meet someone you haven't seen for a while, use phrases such as "Good seeing you again" or "It was nice seeing you." In airline service work, when you greet passengers or customers for the first time, phrases such as these are normally used: Welcome to _____ Air. It's good to have you traveling with us. I am pleased to have you on board today. Welcome aboard.

3. In situations that require meeting people in business related situations, always practice pleasant facial expressions, provide formal greetings, and use polite language.

 Pair Activity

Work with your partner to come up with various greetings and the situations where they are used.

	Greeting	Situation
Example:	How is it going?	At school with a friend

Greeting	Situation

Grammar Practice

The Verb 'Be'

Affirmative/Negative Statements, Subject Pronouns, & Contractions.

The verb 'be' is considered the most irregular verb in English and has the most forms.

Subject Pronoun	Verb be (affirmative)	Verb be (negative)	
I	am	am not	a student.
You	are	are not	from Korea.
He	is	is not	single.
She	is	is not	married.
It	is	is not	difficult.
We	are	are not	working today.
You	are	are not	late.
They	are	are not	very friendly.

In English, every sentence needs a verb. The verb 'be' is often used to describe the condition (mood or the state) of a person or of an event; therefore, there is no action described in the sentence.

* Talking about a person's name or occupation

  I am Susan Smith. I am a professor.

* Talking about a person's age or nationality.

  I am 21 years old. I am from China.

* Talking about a person's personality or mood.

  He is always positive. He is excited to learn English.

* Describing a situation or an event.

   We are late this morning because of the traffic. This place is packed with people.

The verb 'be' is often contracted or shortened in spoken and in written language form.

Subject Pronoun	Verb be (affirmative)	Verb be (negative)	
I	'm (am)	'm not(am not)	a student.
You	're (are)	aren't(are not)	from Korea.
He	's (is)	isn't(is not)	single.
She	's (is)	isn't(is not)	married.
It	's (is)	isn't(is not)	difficult.
We	're (are)	aren't(are not)	working today.
You	're (are)	aren't(are not)	tall.
They	're (are)	aren't(are not)	very friendly.

❙ Photo by Kyle Glenn on Unsplash

Special Reading

How do people around the world greet one another?

We are familiar with a handshake greeting in many Western countries and a head bow greeting in some of the Eastern countries. But did you know there are many other ways to say hello? In Tibet, people stick out their tongue to greet new people. In countries, such as Qatar, Yemen, and Oman, people bump noses for a few friendly taps. You probably have seen people air kiss in various foreign movies. If you have looked at those air kisses carefully, you have probably noticed some people air kiss once, twice, or even up to four on alternating cheeks. One air kiss is common in Argentina, Chile, Columbia, Mexico, and Peru. For countries, such as Spain, Italy, and Paraguay, two is more standard while in Russia and Ukraine, three is common. In some parts of France, people air kiss up to four on alternating cheeks.

In addition to air kisses, in some parts of the world, people rub and sniff faces. In New Zealand, the greeting tradition of 'hongi', which is pressing together of forehead and nose, is practiced as a warm welcome into Maori culture. While the tradition of sniffing and pressing cheeks together seem an intimate gesture, this way of greeting is still common for natives who live in the islands of Polynesia. People in Zimbabwe and Mozambique clap their hands as a way to greet one another, but in Malaysia, a very formal greeting gesture is puting one's hand on his/her heart and giving a nod. Understanding different ways of greeting is a first step in making a meaningful connection when you meet diverse people around the world!

Reading Exercise

Read the text again. Answer the questions.

1. How do people in Tibet greet new people?

_____

_____

_____

2. In which countries do people bump noses to greet one another?

_____

_____

_____

3. Do people in Mexico air kiss?

_____

_____

_____

4. How do people in Zimbabwe greet one another?

_____

_____

_____

5. Which way of greeting surprised you the most? And Why?

_____

_____

_____

Key Expressions to Remember

1. **How do you do? How are you? How are you doing? Hello.**

   안녕하세요.

2. **How is it going? What is up?**

   어떻게 지내니? 잘 지내니?

3. **How is everything? Is everything going OK?**

   잘 지내시죠?

4. **Good morning/afternoon/evening.**

   좋은 아침/오후/저녁 입니다.

5. **I am fine. Thank you for asking. How are you?**

   잘 지냅니다. 물어봐 줘서 고마워요. 잘 지내세요?

6. **It is going fine. Pretty good.**

   잘 지냅니다. 잘 지내요.

7. **It couldn't be better.**

   더 좋을 수 없지요.

8. **I am busy as usual.**

   저는 항상 바빠요.

9. **I can't complain.**

   불만은 없어요..

10. **Nice/good to meet you. I am pleased to meet you. Pleased to meet you.**

    만나서 반가워. 만나서 반갑습니다.

 **Airline Service Expressions**

▸ Greeting Passengers [탑승 인사]

1. Good morning. Welcome aboard.

안녕하십니까? 어서 오십시오.

2. Good afternoon/evening. It's nice to have you on board.

안녕하십니까? 어서 오십시오.

3. May I see your boarding pass, please? Let me see your boarding pass. Will you show me your boarding pass?

탑승권을 확인해 드리겠습니다. 탑승권을 볼 수 있을까요?

4. We have to recheck your boarding pass individually for security.

보안을 위해 한 분씩 탑승권을 재확인하고 있습니다.

5. Thank you for your cooperation.

협조해 주셔서 감사합니다.

6. Please proceed to the other aisle. Please proceed down this aisle.

건너편 통로로 가시면 됩니다. 이쪽 통로로 가시면 됩니다.

▸ At the Check-In Counter [체크인 카운터에서]

7. Where are you going today?

어디까지 가십니까?

8. How many people are in your group?

몇 분이십니까?

9. Where is your final destination for today?

최종 목적지가 어디이십니까?

10. May I please see your ticket and passport?

여권과 항공권을 보여줄 수 있습니까?

 Practice Your English

A. Speaking Activity. Role-play with a partner.

1. You meet your classmate from last year. **Greet your classmate.**

2. You are new to school. **Greet your professor in college.**

3. You are moving into a new dormitory. **Greet your new roommate in college.**

4. You are meeting a passenger at the gate. **Greet your passenger.**

5. You are interviewing for a summer job. **Greet your interviewer.**

B. Writing/Speaking Activity. Create a simple conversation greeting passengers at the gate.

_____

_____

_____

_____

_____

_____

Global English:

**Everyday Conversational
English with Airline
Service Talk**

Unit
02

Introducing yourself and others

자신과 다른 사람들 소개하기

Introducing yourself and others
자신과 다른 사람들 소개하기

Introduction

Learning a new language requires you to know how to introduce yourself and others. There are several ways to introduce yourself depending on different situations. In a formal situation, the kind of information you need to include in your introduction will be different from an informal situation. Here are simple points to remember in order to confidently introduce yourself in English.

• Just say hello and state your name. Then, if applicable, shake hands with the person you are meeting.

Photo by rawpixel on Unsplash

- In formal situations, when you meet someone for the first time, it is best to use formal greetings and to use the person's title (i.e, Mr., Ms., Dr., Professor) with a family last name. Do not use the full name or the first name only if you are meeting someone for the first time.

- Provide some relevant or interesting information about yourself. For example, you can talk about where you are from or where you go to school. If necessary, provide additional information that maybe useful or relevant.

Warm Up Activity

Use the sample personal information card below to introduce David Kim. Then collect information about your partner. Also create your own information card about yourself. Introduce yourself to your partner and introduce your partner to another classmate.

Personal Information Card

Name	David Kim		Name	Partner's Information
Country	South Korea		Country	
Hometown	Busan		Hometown	
Age	21		Age	
Occupation	Student		Occupation	

My name is _____.
I am from _____.
My hometown is _____.
I am _____ years old.
I am a student. (I'm a teacher.)

My partner's name is _____.
He/she is from _____.
His/her hometown is _____.
He/she is _____ years old.
He is a student. (He works at _____.)

 **Conversation 1**

Noah: Hi there. My name is Noah. I am new to this school.

Paul: Hello, Noah. Nice to meet you.

Noah: I recently moved from California. I am studying business administration.
How about you?

Paul: California? I am also from California. That is my hometown. I am studying fashion design now. My plan is to find a job as soon as I graduate.

Noah: How interesting! I wish you all the best.

Paul: Thanks, Noah. I am on my way to my class. See you around the campus.

Noah: Absolutely. Talk to you soon.

 **Conversation 2**

Mr. Lennon: I don't think we have met, Ms. Sommers. I am Tim Lennon. I am
in charge of the marketing department.

Ms. Sommers: Hello, Mr. Lennon. Nice to meet you. I just started work this
week. I am in the sales department. Please call me Sophia.

Mr. Lennon: Nice to meet you, Sophia. Welcome to our company. You can also
call me Tim. If you have any question in the marketing department, don't hesitate to contact me.

Ms. Sommers: Thank you, Tim.

Photo created by yanalya from www.freepik.com

Pointers to Remember

1. In many English-speaking countries, when you meet someone new for the first time, it is polite to shake hands with the person (with both men and women).

2. It is common to state your relationship to the person or the commonality between you and the person, followed by his or her name in the introduction.

3. Although in some countries it may be the norm to ask a person's age when you meet for the first time, in many Western countries it is not polite to ask someone's age.

4. Also, it is always a good idea to say, "Nice to meet you or My pleasure meeting you" after being introduced to someone.

Comprehension Check Exercise

Understand the situations below. Use the expressions provided to introduce yourself and the person in each situation. Add additional phrases and expressions.

1. You are meeting a new professor.

There is someone I would like you to meet. This is Dr. Ward from Hanjin University.

2. You are meeting a new student at school.

Have you met my friend, Ken? This is Ken from Australia.

3. You are meeting a new manager at work.

I would like to introduce the new manager. This is <u>Ms. Park</u>.

4. You are meeting your new neighbor.

Let me introduce my neighbor, <u>James</u>. We live in the same building.

5. You are meeting a new team member.

I want you to meet our new team member, <u>Jenny</u>. This is her first flight to

_____.

Practice the conversations again using your own information.

 **Conversation 3**

Frances: Hi, Kay! How are you?

Kay: Hey, Frances. How is it going?

Frances: Have you met, Yulia? This is Yulia. We are taking a same class. Yulia, this is Kay.

Yulia: Nice to meet you, Kay.

Kay: My pleasure meeting you.

 **Conversation 4**

Gary: Hello, Donna. There is someone I would like you to meet. This is Leslie Kim. She is a new member of our airport ground staff.

Donna: Nice meeting you, Ms. Kim. Welcome to _____ Air. Are you new to this city?

Leslie Kim: Thank you. It's my pleasure. Actually, I am new to the city. I recently moved from _____.

Grammar Practice

The Simple Present: Affirmative and Negative Statements

Add -s or es to the verb with a third person subject he, she, or it. Verbs that end in consonant + -y, change the -y to -i and add -es.

Affirmative Statements	Negative Statements
He works at a bakery.	He doesn't work at a bakery.
My teacher likes apples.	My teacher doesn't like apples.
My sister watches a lot of movies.	My sister doesn't watch a lot of movies.
She studies a lot every day.	She doesn't study a lot every day.
My brother tries to exercise twice a week.	My brother doesn't try to exercise.

Photo by rawpixel.com from Pexels

Special Reading

What are the duties of airport ground staff?

Flight attendants assist airline passengers while traveling in the plane. However, there are other types of airline employees who assist passengers and manage everyday necessary work to make the airport run smoothly. These professionals are called airport ground staff because they help passengers while their plane is grounded at the airport. Passenger service agents are representatives of their airlines, and they are also considered as ground staff. They are responsible for welcoming and assisting passengers at the check-in desks and the boarding gates. Before the flight, passenger service agents verify and assist with passengers' boarding passes, passport documents, and luggage check-ins. When a plane is grounded before it takes off or after it lands, there are airport ground crew employees who load and unload luggage from luggage carriers to and from airplanes. There are also other airport ground crew members that take care of the mechanics of airplanes and conduct security checks at the airport.

 Reading Exercise

Read the text again. Answer the questions.

1. What are the duties of passenger service agents?

_____

_____

_____

_____

2. Who take care of the mechanics of airplanes and conduct security checks at the airport?

_____

_____

_____

_____

3. Do flight attendants assist airline passengers at the airport?

_____

_____

_____

_____

Courtesy of Iclickart

Key Expressions to Remember

1. Have you met, _____? This is _____.

   _____, 만나 보셨습니까? 이분은 _____이세요.

2. Let me introduce my friend, _____.

   제 친구를 소개해 드릴게요.

3. I would like to introduce, _____.

   _____ 소개하고 싶습니다.

4. Please meet, _____.

   여기 _____을 소개합니다.

5. There is someone I would like you to meet. This is _____.

   소개하고 싶은 사람이 있습니다. 이분은 _____입니다.

6. It is a pleasure to meet you. My pleasure meeting you.

   만나서 반갑습니다.

7. It is nice to meet you.

   만나서 반갑습니다.

8. I have heard a lot about you.

   말씀 많이 들었습니다.

9. I don't think we have met.

   우리 아직 못 만나 본 것 같아요.

10. So we finally meet.

    마침내 이렇게 만나 뵙게 됐네요.

Airline Service Expressions

Ticketing at the Check-In Counter [일반 발권]

1. Do you have (a) reservation?

예약은 하셨습니까?

2. Do you have any reservation number?

예약번호는 가지고 계십니까?

3. Would you like to buy/purchase a ticket?

항공권을 구입하십니까?

4. Would you like to go today? Where would you like to go?

오늘 출발하십니까? 어디까지 가십니까?

| Photo by H W on Unsplash

5. **Would you like to buy a one-way ticket or round-trip?**

   항공권 구입은 편도이십니까? 아니시면 왕복이십니까?

6. **Excuse me, could you show me your passport?**

   실례합니다, 여권을 보여 주시겠습니까?

7. **I would like to double-check your name with the passport.**

   여권으로 이름을 다시 확인하고 싶습니다.

8. **Could you please confirm the reservation?**

   다시 한번 예약을 확인해 주시겠습니까?

9. **How would like to pay? What would like to pay with?**

   지불은 어떻게/무엇으로 하시겠습니까?

10. **We accept a credit card, the Korean Won, the Japanese Yen, and the US dollar.**

    신용 카드, 원화, 엔화, 미국 달러로 지불 가능합니다.

Practice Your English

A. Speaking Activity. Work with a partner to understand each situation below and practice the conversation together. Introduce your partner to the class using the expression of your choice.

1. You meet a school friend. Introduce your school friend to your best friend.

   _____

   _____

   _____

2. You meet your college professor at a mall. Introduce the professor to your father and vice versa.

_____

_____

_____

_____

3. You meet your coworker at a store. Introduce your coworker to your sister.

_____

_____

_____

_____

4. You meet a friend at the library. Introduce introduce him/her to your girl/boyfriend.

_____

_____

_____

_____

B. Small Group Activity. Form a group of 5-6 students. Have a student introduce a person next to him/her. Do this until everyone has been introduced.

A: _____, this is my friend, _____. We are both from _____.

    This is _____.

B: Great to meet you, _____.

C: My pleasure meeting you, too.

C. Speaking Activity. Do a role - play being a customer and a ground staff member at the ticket counter. Use appropriate expressions to ask and answer questions about making a reservation. Create a meaningful conversation.

A: Good morning, sir. Do you have a reservation?

B: No, I don't. Is there a flight to _____ this afternoon?

Global English:

Everyday Conversational English with Airline Service Talk

Unit
0 3

Starting and Keeping
a Conversation
대화를 시작하고 유지하기

Starting and Keeping a Conversation
대화를 시작하고 유지하기

Introduction

Striking a conversation with a stranger can be a difficult task for many people. However, for English language learners, it can be even more difficult. In this unit, students will learn basic conversational techniques that will be useful to strike a conversation in English and to keep the conversation going.

One way to start a conversation is to make small talk. Small talk is defined as an informal, friendly conversation about unimportant matters or subjects before the main event (i.e., meetings, special events, or interviews). The conversation, sometimes called a chit-chat, usually takes place with strangers or people you have not seen for a long time. People make small talk to fill an uncomfortable silence and to avoid awkwardness when talking with strangers. For others, they make small talk in order to be polite. It can be considered as rude if you do not make any effort to meet or to talk to people during a party or an event.

▌Photo by Helena Lopes on Unsplash

Small Talk Topics: Conversation Starters

See the common topics and expressions below.

1. Talking about the weather (날씨에 대해 말하기)

* Today is a beautiful day, isn't it?

* What a rainy day today! I am glad we are inside.

* It looks like it is going to snow.

* I hear we are going to have a storm this weekend.

* Are you enjoying this weather?

2. Talking about current events (현재 뉴스에 대해 말하기)

* Did you watch the game yesterday?

* How about the match yesterday?

* I can't believe about the news on _____.

3. At school or at work (학교 또는 직장에서)

* Do you have any plans for the weekend?

* We are busy today, aren't we?

* How long have you been working here?

* What are you studying?

* I can use a cup of coffee now. How about you?

4. At a social event (행사에서)

* Are you enjoying yourself?

* What a nice party! Isn't it?

* I am Joey's friend, _____. What is your name?

* I like your shoes. They look nice.

* Have you tried this dish?

5. **Waiting somewhere** (어디에서 기다리고 있을 때)

    * What a nice day today.

    * I picked a wrong day to come. How long have you been waiting?

    * The bus must be running late today.

    * Do you have the time?

    * How is it going?

Warm Up Activity

Start the conversations using the following topics.

1. Talking about the weather (날씨에 대해 말하기)

_____

_____

_____

_____

2. Talking about current events (현재 뉴스에 대해 말하기)

_____

_____

_____

_____

3. Finding commonalities at school or at work (학교 또는 직장에서 공통점 찾기)

_____

_____

_____

_____

4. Asking questions at a social event (행사에서 질문하기)

_____

_____

_____

_____

5. Waiting somewhere (어디에서 기다리고 있을 때)

_____

_____

_____

_____

Conversation 1

A: Excuse me, do you know what time it is?

B: It is 15 minutes past 8 a.m.

A: Wow. The bus is running late this morning.

B: I know. I have been waiting 20 minutes now.

A: By the way, I am new to this neighborhood. My name is Kenny.

B: Hi, my name is April. I have lived here for about a year now. Welcome.

A: Thanks, April. I sure hope the bus arrives soon.

B: Me too.

Conversation 2

A: It is such a nice day today. I hear it is going to be very warm this weekend.

B: I know. Are you doing anything special this weekend?

A: Yes, I am watching my brother's game this weekend.

B: That is nice. What sport does he play?

A: He plays baseball for his high school. This is his last game for the season.

B: Well, that is good that the weather will be nice.

A: How about you? Do you have any plans?

B: Actually, I am working this weekend. We have a project due next Monday.

A: Good luck with your project!

Photo by nappy from Pexels

✎ Comprehension Check Exercise

Complete each conversation with the appropriate starter.

• At a social event

1. A: _____

   B: Thank you! I bought them online.

• Waiting somewhere

2. A: _____

   B: I have been waiting about 15 minutes.

• Talking about current events

3. A: _____

   B: Yes, I can't believe _____ won last night. It was amazing.

• At school or at work

4. A: _____

   B: I am not sure yet. Perhaps we might watch a movie this weekend. How about you?

• Talking about the weather

5. A: _____

   B: Yes, it is so nice today. I can't wait to go outside.

Pointers to Remember

1. In small talk, approach the people you want to talk to and introduce yourself.

2. Have simple expressions ready to use. It can be difficult to start a conversation with a new person. Know some of the key expressions in general topics, such as "Are you enjoying the weather?" "What a lovely day today!" and "How do you like _____?"

3. Be an observer and be a good listener. Be ready to receive and give compliments. Look at your partner and find something nice to compliment him/her on. For example, saying something nice about his/her clothes is a good start.

4. Find common interests with your speaking partner. This helps both parties at ease when doing small talk.

5. Asking questions is one of the best ways to start and to maintain an interesting conversation.

6. Be interested in the conversation by showing attention and agreement. Some of the reaction expressions include: Really? How interesting. Wow! I didn't know. So do I! It sure is.

Pair Activity

Asking Follow-Up Questions.

Asking questions is one of the best ways to start a conversation. Use the following statements below to create follow-up questions. Then do a role-play with your partner. Take turns asking and answering questions.

A. I missed my English class yesterday.

_____

_____

_____

B. I saw a movie this weekend.

_____

_____

_____

C. My family moved to a new country this summer.

_____

_____

_____

D. I have a new professor in my English class.

_____

_____

_____

_____

Group Activity

Conversational Techniques

Read the conversation and identify (or underline) some of the conversational techniques used in the conversation.

A: What do you currently do?

B: I am a student.

A: Really? What are you studying?

B: I am studying marketing and Korean language. How about you? What is your profession?

A: I am a flight attendant.

B: Are you? It must be nice to travel many different places.

A: It sure is. Last week I traveled to Hong Kong and Vietnam for work.

B: Hong Kong? I am from Hong Kong. It is my hometown.

A: How interesting! I really enjoyed the place. I want to visit again because I got to stay for only one day.

B: That was a short visit. I will be happy to tell you some of the places you can visit next time.

A: That sounds great!

See the conversational techniques below and write appropriate expressions from the conversation above.

1. Asking questions _____

2. Showing interest _____

3. Agreeing _____

4. Using echo question _____

5. Using echo word _____

(*See Appendix 5 for answers.)

Grammar Practice

Yes/No Questions and Wh-Questions

Simple Yes/No Questions with Be Verbs

We create simple yes/no questions by inverting the order of subject and the "to be" verb.

Yes/No Questions	Affirmative Statements
Am I a student?	I am a student.
Are you happy?	You are happy.
Is she working today?	She is working today.
Are they learning English?	They are learning English.
Were you late this morning?	You were late this morning.
Am I walking too fast?	I am walking too fast.
Is my brother taller than me?	My brother is taller than me.
Was he exercising this morning?	He was exercising this morning.

Yes/No Questions with Helping Verbs

In creating yes/no questions, helping verbs or auxiliary verbs come before the subject. Generally, these questions ask for yes or no response with additional information. Ex: Do you like classical music? Yes, I really enjoy listening to classical music.

의문문에서는, 조동사가 주어 앞에 온다. 대체로, 이러한 의문문은 네 또는 아니오 외의 정보에 대해서도 질문 한다. 예시: 클래식 음악을 좋아하는가? 네, 저는 클래식 음악을 듣는 것을 좋아합니다.

Yes/No Questions With Helping Verbs	Affirmative Statements
Do you like classical music?	You like classical music.
Do you live in New York?	You live in New York.
Can I speak two languages?	I can speak two languages.
Have you visited me last year?	You have visited me last year.
Should I leave my bag here?	I should leave my bag here.
Will you have lunch with me today?	You will have lunch with me today.

Wh-Questions with Be Verbs

We use wh-questions to ask for specific information. The most common wh-question words are: what, who, where, when, why, and how.

Question Word	Be Verb	Subject
What	is	the question?
Who	is	the professor?
Where	are	my shoes?
When	is	the meeting?
Why	is	this book special?
How	are	the dishes?

Key Expressions to Remember

1. **Today is a beautiful day.**

   오늘은 화창한 날입니다.

2. **Do you have any plans for the weekend?**

   주말에 어떤 계획이 있나요?

3. **Do you have the time?**

   몇 시인지 아시나요?

4. **How is it going?**

   어떻게 잘 지내요?

5. **I am doing great.**

   잘 지내고 있어요.

6. **I am studying business.**

   사업을 공부하고 있습니다.

7. **Are you enjoying this weather?**

   이 날씨를 즐기고 있습니까?

8. **What are you studying?**

   어떤 공부를 하고 있어요?

9. **What do you do?**

   당신의 직업은 무엇인가요?

10. **I am a student.**

    저는 학생입니다.

Airline Service Expressions

Baggage Check at the Check-In Counter [체크인 카운터에서 수하물 확인]

1. Do you have any baggage to check? Would you like to check in any luggage?

   맡기실 짐은 있으십니까?

2. How many bags/suitcases will you be checking in today?

   오늘 맡기실 짐은 전부 몇 개이십니까?

3. Please put your baggage on the scale.

   맡기실 짐은 저울에 올려 주시기 바랍니다.

4. Sorry, but could you put it one by one please.

   죄송합니다만, 하나씩 올려 주시기 바랍니다.

Courtesy of Pexels

5. **Please have your baggage laid down on the belt.**

   짐은 벨트에 눕혀 주시겠습니까?

6. **Whose bag is this?**

   이 짐은 어느 분 짐이십니까?

7. **Mr./Mrs. _____, you have checked _____ baggage to _____.**

   _____손님, _____까지 짐 _____개를 부치셨습니다.

8. **Please attach a name tag to your luggage.**

   손님 짐에 이름표를 달아 주시기 바랍니다.

9. **Your baggage claim tags are attached to the back of the ticket here.**

   짐표는 항공권 뒷면에 붙여 두겠습니다.

10. **Please keep the tags with you.**

    짐표를 잘 보관 하십시오.

Courtesy of Pexels

Practice Your English

A. Speaking Activity. Take turns starting a conversation by asking a question to your partner. Maintain each conversation by using conversational techniques such as asking follow-up questions, showing interests and agreements, and using echo-words or questions.

1. What do you currently do?

_____

_____

_____

2. Where is your hometown?

_____

_____

_____

3. What are you doing this weekend?

_____

_____

_____

4. Have you ever been abroad?

_____

_____

_____

5. Do you like watching movies?

_____

_____

_____

6. What kind of music do you like?

_____

_____

_____

7. What did you do in the summer/winter vacation?

_____

_____

_____

8. How do you spend your free time?

_____

_____

_____

9. Where are you flying today?

_____

_____

_____

10. How did you get here?

_____

_____

_____

B. Group Activity. Play a guessing game. Select a student to think of a famous person. Have other students ask questions to guess the name of the person.

> **Example:** Famous Soccer Player _____
>
> Is he tall?
> Does he play for _____?
> Where is he from _____?
> Did he ever win the World Cup?

1. _____

   _____

2. _____

   _____

3. _____

   _____

4. _____

   _____

5. _____

   _____

6. _____

   _____

7. _____

   _____

8. _____

   _____

Global English :

Everyday Conversational English with Airline Service Talk

Unit
04

Talking about habits
and routines

습관과 일상에 대해 말하기

Talking about habits and routines
습관과 일상에 대해 말하기

 Introduction

In English, when we talk about habitual activities or actions that do not often change, we use the simple present tense. These habitual activities indicate that we do them on a regular basis. Think of some of the daily activities that you do at home, at work, or at school. How often do you do them? We also use the simple present tense to talk about general facts or conditions about ourselves.

▌ Photo by rawpixel.com from Pexels

Warm Up Activity

See the occupations below and match them according to what the people do. Then with the pertinent information, create sentences using the correct verb tense forms.

Example: A flight attendant provides in-flight service to airline passengers.

1. A flight attendant	a. take care of sick people
2. A nurse	b. build computer programs
3. Lawyers	c. play a character in a movie
4. Computer engineers	d. plan weddings for brides and grooms
5. An actor	e. help customers with reservations
6. Artists	f. practice law
7. Air traffic controllers	g. drive passengers to destinations
8. Wedding planners	h. provide in-flight service
9. Bus drivers	i. make art
10. A hotel receptionist	k. direct airplanes

1. _____
2. _____
3. _____
4. _____
5. _____
6. _____
7. _____
8. _____
9. _____
10. _____

 **Conversation 1**

Michelle: Hi Will, where are you going this morning?

Will: I am on my way to the gym. I have a swimming class.

Michelle: You are so diligent! How often do you swim?

Will: I swim twice a week, but I try to go to the gym every day. I do various workouts.

Michelle: No wonder you look so fit!

Will: Thanks, Michelle. Do you want to join our gym? My gym is great, and they are always looking for new members. They are offering discounts these days.

Michelle: Sure, I'll think about it. Thanks for the information.

Photo by Curtis MacNewton on Unsplash

 **Conversation 2**

Nikki: Are you free this weekend? Do you want to watch the new Avengers movie?

Julia: Sure, that sounds fun. But I haven't watched any of the Avengers series. Is that going to be a problem?

Nikki: Really? I can't believe you haven't watched any of it. But it should be okay. I guess I watch movies pretty often.

Julia: I am more of a reader. I always read a new book every month. How often do you watch a movie?

Nikki: I watch a movie whenever I have time. I try to watch at least two or three movies every month.

Julia: Wow! You do watch movies often. I want to try something new. I think it will be fun to watch the movie this weekend.

Nikki: Okay. Let me tell you something about the series, so it is not so confusing to you.

Grammar Practice

Adverbs of Frequency

Adverbs of frequency tell how often something happens. They often come between the subject and the verb. To emphasize, some adverbs of frequency come at the beginning or at the end of a sentence. Adverbs of frequency come after the 'be' verbs.*

빈도부사는 무언가가 얼마나 자주 발생 하는지를 알려준다. 빈도부사는 목적어와 동사 사이에서 자주 볼 수 있다. 강조를 위해, 몇몇 빈도부사는 문장의 시작이나 끝에 위치한다. 빈도부사는 'be'동사 다음에 온다.

How often do you _____ ? How often do you exercise?

얼마나 자주 _____ 하는가? 얼마나 자주 운동 하는가?

Do you ever go to a concert?

혹시 콘서트에 가세요?

always 항상	almost always 거의 항상	usually 대체로	often/ frequently 자주/빈번하게	some-times 때때로	seldom/ rarely 드물게/거의 ~않다	never 절대로
100%	90-70%	70-60%	60-50%	50-40%	30-10%	0%

In many cases, frequency and time expressions come at the end of a sentence. However, sometimes frequency and time expressions can come at the beginning of a sentence. Make sure to use a comma (,) after the expressions at the beginning of a sentence.

Ex: I exercise twice a week. I try to exercise every evening. Twice a week, I eat out with my family.

대부분의 경우에, 빈도와 시간을 나타내는 표현들은 문장의 마지막에 위치한다. 그러나 빈도와 시간을 나타내는 표현들이 가끔씩 문장의 시작에 올 때가 있다. 문장 처음에 그러한 표현들이 올 때는 표현 뒤에 쉼표(,)를 사용하는 것을 잊어서는 안 된다.

예시: 나는 일주일에 두 번 운동한다. 나는 매일 저녁에 운동을 하려고 노력한다. 일주일에 두 번, 나는 가족들과 외식을 한다.

Frequency Expressions 빈도를 나타내는 표현 **all the time** 항상	Time Expressions 시간을 나타내는 표현 **in + the morning** 아침에
once a week / month / year 일주일에 한번 / 한 달에 한번 / 일 년에 한번	in + the afternoon 오후에
twice a week / month / year 2주에 한번 / 2달에 한번 / 2년에 한번	in + the evening 저녁에
three times a week / month / year 일주일에 3번 / 한 달에 3번 / 일 년에 3번	in + January 1월에
every morning / afternoon / evening / night 매일 아침 / 매일 오후 / 매일 저녁 / 매일 밤	in + 1996 1996년에
every day / week / year 매일 / 매주 / 매년	in + the summer / fall / winter / spring 여름에 / 가을에 / 겨울에 / 봄에
every summer / winter / spring / fall 매년 여름 / 매년 겨울 / 매년 봄 / 매년 가을	on + Monday(s) / weekends / May 1 월요일마다 / 주말마다 / 매년 5월 1일마다
	at + night / noon / 10:00 밤에 / 정오에 / 10시에

Pointers to Remember

We use frequency adverbs and expressions to talk about how often an action or an event occurs. We use phrases such as 'How often...' or 'Do you ever...' when asking questions.

Comprehension Check Exercise

A. Match the frequency adverbs with the frequency expressions.

Frequency Adverbs	Frequency Expressions
1. always	a. generally
2. almost always	b. hardly ever
3. usually	c. all the time
4. often	d. many times
5. sometimes	e. not at all
6. seldom	f. once in a while
7. never	g. frequently

B. Complete the sentences with a frequency or a time expression.

1. My sister _____ gets up at 6:00 in the morning.

2. My brother _____ skips breakfast. But he _____ skips dinner at home.

3. I go to school _____ because I _____ have a class Monday, Wednesday, and Friday morning.

4. My cat _____ takes a nap _____.

5. My mother prepares dinner for us _____. She _____ makes Korean food, which is my favorite.

6. My dad comes home _____ and _____ plays us. Even though he works hard, he is _____ tired.

💬 Pair Activity

Do you have a healthy lifestyle? Do you do any of these activities?

Check Yes or No. Then ask your partner if he or she does any of these activities.

> **Example:** A: Do you exercise every day?
> B: Not really. But I exercise three times a week. How about you?

	Yes	No
1. Exercise every day	_____	_____
2. Drink three or more coffee drinks every day	_____	_____
3. Eat fast food or instant food every day	_____	_____
4. Eat fruit and vegetables every day	_____	_____
5. Eat red meat every day	_____	_____
6. Skip meals	_____	_____
7. Eat junk food every day	_____	_____
8. Play computer games more than 3 hours	_____	_____
9. Overeat every meal	_____	_____
10. Go to bed late	_____	_____
11. Eat home cooked meals	_____	_____
12. Take vitamins	_____	_____

1. _____
2. _____
3. _____
4. _____
5. _____
6. _____
7. _____
8. _____
9. _____
10. _____
11. _____
12. _____

Photo by Trang Doan from Pexels

Class Activity

Share your information with the class.

Have students share their information with the rest of the class. Tell the class whether you and your partner have a healthy life style.

> **Example:** I don't have a healthy life style. I eat too much junk food. My partner has a healthy life style. He doesn't eat fast food, and he exercises three times a week.

_____

_____

_____

_____

_____

_____

Special Reading

What are some interesting habits of famous people?

Everyone has a habit or two that can be considered odd. Some habits, such as turning lights on when sleeping or listening to music while cleaning, could be considered normal. However, have you heard of habits such as eating bugs for protein and drinking salt water after a good workout? Those are exactly the habits that some famous people do. Angelina Jolie has stated in the past that she sometimes eats bugs because she learned that bugs have lots of protein. Jessica Alba who is an American actress and a businesswoman has expressed that she enjoys drinking salt water after difficult workouts.

Furthermore, it was reported that creative genius, Steve Jobs, often ate the same food for many days in a row if he liked a certain kind of food. He was also known for eating so many carrots because he liked them so much. The American billionaire, Warren Buffet has stated that he drinks at least five cans of Coca-Cola each day as a habit to maintain good health at 86. There are other interesting habits of famous people. Some of these habits include eating jalapenos every day, brushing teeth with strawberries, and drinking over 40 cups of coffee each day. Do any of these habits surprise you?

Reading Exercise

Read the text again. Write T (True) or F (False) for each statement.

1. _____ Jessica Alba eats bugs because she learned that bugs have lots of protein.

2. _____ Warren Buffet drinks at least 7 cans of Coca-Cola each day.

3. _____ Steve Jobs was known for eating so many carrots.

4. _____ Angelina Jolie drinks salt water after a difficult workout.

5. _____ Steve Jobs often ate the same food for many days in a row if he liked them.

Group Activity

Do you have a habit that is considered odd?

_____

_____

_____

_____

_____

_____

_____

_____

_____

Key Expressions to Remember

1. What do you do in your free time?

여가 시간에는 무엇을 합니까?

2. What do you do for fun?

취미 생활이 뭐예요?

3. What is your hobby?

당신의 취미는 무엇입니까?

4. How often do you watch it?

얼마나 자주 시청하나요?

5. Do you exercise often?

자주 운동합니까?

6. Are you free this weekend?

이번 주말에 시간 있으세요?

7. I enjoy reading books.

저는 책을 읽는 것을 즐깁니다.

8. I usually meet friends on weekends.

저는 보통 주말에 친구들을 만나요.

9. I exercise twice a week.

저는 일주일에 두 번 운동을 합니다.

10. I am a flight attendant.

저는 승무원 입니다.

Airline Service Expressions

Asking about Seating Arrangement at the Check-In Counter
[체크인 카운터에서 좌석 배치에 관한 문의]

1. **Do you have any preference for a certain seat?**

   원하시는 좌석은 있습니까?

2. **Would you like a window seat or an aisle seat?**

   통로하고 창가 쪽 중 어느 쪽이 좋으십니까?

3. **Would you like to sit together? Would you like to sit next to each other?**

   함께 나란히 앉으실 수 있는 좌석으로 괜찮으시겠습니까?

4. **If you don't mind, how about an aisle seat in the back?**

   혹시 괜찮으시면 뒤쪽 통로 자리로 드리면 어떨까요?

5. **Let me find it for you. Please wait for a moment.**

   찾아보겠습니다. 잠시만 기다려 주세요.

6. **You have already pre-assigned to 33A, which is a window seat. Is this Ok for you?**

   현재 창가 쪽 자리인 33A로 사전 지정하셨는데, 그대로 드려도 괜찮겠습니까?

7. **Today's seats are arranged 3-4-3, and which side would you prefer?**

   오늘 이 비행기 좌석 배치는 3-4-3으로 되어 있습니다만, 어느 쪽으로 하시겠습니까?

8. **We ran out of seats that you can sit next to each other.**

   현재 나란히 같이 앉으실 수 있는 좌석은 없습니다.

9. **How about sitting back and forth?** 앞뒤로 나란한 좌석은 어떠신지요?

10. **How about seats on the 1st floor?** 1층 좌석은 어떠시겠습니까?

Practice Your English

A. Speaking Activity 1. Use the time and frequency expressions below and make true statements about yourself. Then share your statements with your partner.

> **Example:** once a year
>   You: My parents and I take a vacation once a year.

1. once a year

2. every Friday

3. twice a week

4. every week

5. on Saturday mornings

6. in May

7. in the summer

8. hardly ever

9. all the time

10. on my birthday

1. _____

2. _____

3. _____

4. _____

5. _____

6. _____

7. _____

8. _____

9. _____

10. _____

B. Speaking Activity 2. Create a weekly schedule with your information. Use the schedule information to ask and to answer questions using frequency and time expressions.

For example: How often do you exercise? When do you have classes?

I go grocery shopping on Saturday mornings.

Weekly Schedule

Time	Monday	Tuesday	Wednesday	Thursday	Friday	Saturday

Global English :

Everyday Conversational
English with Airline
Service Talk

Unit
05

Describing people
사람들 묘사하기

Describing people
사람들 묘사하기

 Introduction

There are many ways to describe people. We can describe people on their physical appearance, mannerism, character trait, and emotional state. Physical appearance is what people look like on the outside. Mannerisms are the ways how people act or behave. Character traits demonstrate people's personality. Emotional states are what and how people feel at a certain moment. It is good to use a variety of adjectives when describing people in English.

Warm Up Activity

What are the different ways to describe people? See the sentences below and match them according to correct contexts: Write (P) for physical appearance, (M) for mannerism, (C) for character trait, and (E) for emotion. Also circle the adjective words.

1. Students are energetic. _____

2. My classmates are smart. _____

3. Mr. Kim is happy this morning. _____

4. I bite my fingernails when I'm nervous. _____

5. People say I am talkative. _____

6. My mother has good manners. _____

7. The new actor is gorgeous. _____

8. She looks thin and fit. _____

9. I have blond hair. _____

10. The ground staff provided friendly service. _____

Conversation 1

Dana: Hi Clark. Have you seen Anna? She is the new member of our club?

Clark: I haven't met her. What does she look like?

Dana: She is medium height and thin. She has dark brown hair and quite pretty.

Clark: Is that her behind Tom? She is talking to Ari.

Dana: Who is Tom?

Clark: Tom is also new. He is that tall guy with blond hair. He is wearing a leather jacket.

 **Conversation 2**

Interviewer: How would your friends describe you?

Interviewee: I believe my friends would describe me as a responsible and committed person. They know that I am a hard working individual who always gives her best. In college, I received positive compliments from fellow classmates and professors because of my class projects and presentations.

Interviewer: How about your coworkers? How would they describe you?

Interviewee: In my previous job, I worked as a server in a family restaurant. My job required me to work with various team members. So it was very important for all of us to work cooperatively. My coworkers would say that I was a good team player because I was always willing to help.

Comprehension Check Exercise

A. Select the appropriate adjective words in the box to complete the sentences.

polite	friendly	active	gorgeous	cheerful	calm
shy	bright	creative	muscular	graceful	tall

1. My sister is _____ and slim. People think she is a model.

2. Albert is my best friend who is very _____. He always comes up with interesting ideas.

3. I like my teacher. She is _____ and intelligent.

4. Did you watch the show? The lead ballet dancer is _____ and talented.

5. Have you been working out? You look _____.

6. The new restaurant is excellent. The food is great and the waiters are

_____.

7. Who is the new girl? She looks _____.

8. During unexpected situations, it is important for everyone to remain

_____.

9. I am quite busy these days. I am _____ at school and at work.

10. My best friend is _____. He doesn't enjoy meeting new people.

B. Now use the appropriate adjective words in the box to ask a partner questions.

polite	friendly	active	gorgeous	cheerful	calm
shy	bright	creative	muscular	graceful	tall

Example: You: Are you active?

Your Partner: Yes, I am. I am busy with school activities.

_____

_____

_____

_____

_____

_____

_____

Pair Activity

Think of celebrities that you like. Ask and answer questions about the celebrities you and your partner like.

> **Example:** You: Who is your favorite actor?
>
> Your Partner: My favorite actor is Robert Downing Jr.
>
> You: Why do you like him?
>
> Your Partner: I think he is handsome. He is also talented.

_____

_____

_____

_____

_____

_____

_____

_____

_____

_____

_____

_____

Pointers to Remember

When describing people, it is important to be tactful and polite. Some people are sensitive about their appearance, so be careful when selecting words to describe them. Some of the words that should be avoided when describing people are "ugly", "fat", "skinny", and "old". Instead of saying someone is fat, you can say someone is a bit heavy or slightly overweight. There is always a nicer way to describe someone, so always select more appropriate words.

Alterative words to "fat" -
curvy / big built / heavy / plump / overweight / chubby

Alternative words to "skinny"
slim / slender / petite (especially for women)

Alternative words to "old"
elderly (65+) / senior citizen / middle-aged (50 +)

Grammar Practice

Adjectives

Adjectives are words that describe or modify a person, a place, or a thing in the sentence. The articles — a, an, and the — often precede adjectives.

* **The adjective is placed before a noun.**

  My grandparents live in a traditional house.

* **The adjective comes after the verb be (am, is, are).**

  The weather is warm today.

* **Use words such as very, so, extremely to make the adjective stronger. These words come before most adjectives.**

  My new puppy is extremely cute.

* **The ending of an adjective always remains the same. Do not put "s" on the adjective when subject is singular or plural.**

  I moved to a different place. I have lived in many different (not differents) places.

* **The adjective comes after the linking verb or a verb that has to do with the five human senses, look/feel/smell/taste/sound.**

  (i.e., Why do you look tired today?)

🎙 **Speaking Activity**

Do show and tell. Bring a picture of your family. Describe your family to your partner.

> **example:** This is a picture of my family. My dad is tall and handsome.
> My mom is pretty and nice. My sister is adorable and cute. She
> makes everyone smile.

_____

_____

_____

_____

_____

_____

Courtesy of Iclickart

Special Reading

What are the benefits of VIP lounges at the airport?

Many travelers spend a lot of time at the airport. This may be due to layovers, connecting flights, flight delays, or cancellations of flights. If travelers have access to VIP or airport lounges at the airport, it helps to make traveling more enjoyable. Airport lounges provide comfortable spaces for travelers to enjoy quiet time at the airport. There are sofas and chairs for travelers to relax and to do any business and school related work when necessary. Having free and fast WiFi is basic. Airport lounges also provide equipment to print boarding passes and to charge any phone or computer devices. One of the best perks of airport lounges is the complimentary beverage and food services for their users. Unfortunately, not everyone has access to airport lounges. However, for those who do have access can relax and indulge in tasty snacks and drinks as well as keep themselves productive while waiting for their next flights.

Reading Exercise

Read the text again. Answer the following questions?

1. Does everyone have access to airport or VIP lounges?

_____

_____

2. What kind of services do airport lounges provide for the users?

_____

_____

3. Do airport lounges provide complimentary drinks and snacks?

_____

_____

Photo by mark chaves on Unsplash

Key Expressions to Remember

1. **How would you describe yourself?**

   당신을 어떻게 표현 하시겠습니까?

2. **How would your friends describe you?**

   친구들이 당신을 어떻게 표현 하시겠습니까?

3. **What does he look like?**

   그는 어떻게 생겼나요?

4. **How is her personality?**

   그녀의 성격은 어때요?

5. **I believe I am a kind person.**

   저는 친절한 사람이라고 믿습니다.

6. **My friends describe me as a positive person.**

   친구들은 저를 긍정적인 사람으로 묘사합니다.

7. **I see myself as an outgoing person.**

   저는 제 자신을 사교적인 사람이라고 생각합니다.

8. **She is tall and slim.**

   그녀는 키가 크고 날씬합니다.

9. **He is muscular and attractive.**

   그는 근육질이고 매력적입니다.

10. **She is understanding and compassionate.**

    그녀는 이해심과 배려심이 강합니다.

Airline Service Expressions

At the VIP Lounge [VIP 라운지 방문]

1. **Welcome to _____'s VIP lounge.**
   _____ VIP 라운지에 오신 것을 환영합니다.

2. **Would you show me your boarding pass?**
   탑승권을 보여 주시겠습니까?

3. **You are free to enter the lounge.**
   라운지에 자유롭게 입장하셔도 좋습니다.

4. **Do you have any membership card?**
   회원 카드가 있으십니까?

5. **I am sorry, but only one passenger can use this lounge.**
   죄송하지만, 손님 한 분만 이용 가능합니다.

6. **We are very sorry, but you are not able to use the lounge.**
   대단히 죄송하오나, 손님의 경우에는 라운지 사용이 불가합니다.

7. **Would you please put your luggage in the coatroom?**
   짐은 여기 COAT ROOM안에 넣어 주시겠습니까?

8. **Could you take any valuable item with you?**
   귀중품은 손님께서 직접 소지해 주시겠습니까?

9. **You can use the computer in front of the desk anytime.**
   안내 DESK앞 컴퓨터는 자유롭게 사용하실 수 있습니다.

10. **Please enjoy the lounge. Do you have any questions?**
    라운지를 즐기십시오. 질문 있으세요?

Practice Your English

A. Speaking Activity 1. What is important to you when you make friends? Write down characteristics that are important to you. Then share them with your partner.

> **Example:** It is important my friends are kind and friendly. I also want
>
> them to be loyal. How about you?

_____

_____

_____

_____

_____

_____

_____

_____

B. Writing/Speaking Activity 2. Describe your best friend. Use the following questions to compose a short paragraph about your best friend.

1. What is his/her name?

2. How tall is he/she?

3. What color is his/her hair?

4. What does he/she look like?

5. Is he/she slim?

6. Is he/she good looking?

7. How is his/her personality?

8. What do you like about him or her?

9. How did you meet him/her?

10. How are you similar or different?

Photo by Omar Lopez on Unsplash

Global English:
Everyday Conversational English with Airline Service Talk

Unit
06

Talking about vacation
휴가에 대해 말하기

Talking about vacation
휴가에 대해 말하기

 Introduction

There are so many different ways to talk about vacation. We can talk about a vacation that we have already taken or that we dream of taking in the future. Talking about vacation is a popular topic in an English language classroom. After all, there are many types of vacation and different activities people do when they are on their vacation. This chapter will provide lots of opportunities for students to talk about various vacation trips and different ways people enjoy their vacation.

Photo by Link Hoang on Unsplash

Warm Up Activity

What kind of activities people do when they are on vacation? See the activities below and check the activities you have done. Then share what you have done with your partner.

	Yes	No
A. fishing	_____	_____
B. shopping	_____	_____
C. sightseeing	_____	_____
D. jet skiing	_____	_____
E. rock climbing	_____	_____
F. bike riding	_____	_____
G. hiking	_____	_____
H. scuba diving	_____	_____
I. sailing	_____	_____
J. camping	_____	_____
K. kayaking	_____	_____
L. sun bathing	_____	_____
M. bungee jumping	_____	_____
O. skiing/snow boarding	_____	_____

> **Example:** You: I went sightseeing in Canada this summer.
>
> Your Partner: Wow in Canada! How was it?

_____

_____

_____

_____

 **Conversation 1**

Edward: Hi Jean! Long time no see. How was your winter vacation?

Jean: Hello Edward. It was great! I went skiing in Colorado with my family.

Edward: Really? How was it?

Jean: It was awesome. It actually snowed while we were skiing, so the mountains were more beautiful.

Edward: I bet. Are you good at skiing?

Jean: I am okay. I took a couple of lessons many years ago. I think I will always remain a beginner because I am a careful skier. How about you? What did you do over the winter vacation?

Edward: Well, I worked most of the time. But I took a short vacation. I just relaxed and visited art galleries.

Jean: That actually sounds fun. I am tired from traveling, so I just want to relax now.

 Conversation 2

Sam: What are you doing for the summer? Do you have any summer vacation plans?

Michelle: I am not sure yet. But my sister and I are thinking about traveling to New York for a week.

Sam: That sounds good. But why New York?

Michelle: My sister is an art student, so she wants to visit lots of art galleries there. I have never visited the East Coast before, so I would like to visit New York. What about you? What is your plan for the summer?

Sam: My friend is getting married in California in July. So I am planning to take a vacation around that time to visit Los Angeles and San Francisco.

Michelle: Really? You know I used to live in San Francisco when I was young.

Sam: Oh yeah? I did not know that.

Michelle: I can tell you where to visit in San Francisco. It is a beautiful city. I definitely recommend the Golden Gate Bridge.

 Conversation 3

Ben: Hi Jamie! How was your summer?

Jamie: Hey Ben! It was alright. I studied most of the time.

Ben: So did I! I had to take additional classes over the summer. So I didn't have any time for a real vacation.

Jamie: Me too. But I spent one weekend at a friend's beach house.

Ben: So did I! Who is your friend?

Jamie: Her name is Katy. What is your friend's name?

Ben: No way! Her name is Katy, too.

Pair Activity

Practice each conversation again. You can also use your own stories or different ideas.

 Comprehension Check Exercise

Complete the sentences using the appropriate verbs from the box. Please change the tense forms when necessary.

go	spend	meet	use	plan
buy	send	take	stay	visit

1. I _____ one weekend at a friend's beach house last summer.

2. My sister and I _____ to live in San Francisco when we were young.

3. We _____ to visit New York this upcoming summer.

4. I _____ snow boarding with my family last winter.

5. We usually _____ art galleries and museums when we travel.

6. My sister _____ lots of photos while we were sightseeing.

7. I _____ an interesting person while visiting Canada.

8. My family and I usually _____ in a nice hotel.

9. My friend _____ me lots of photos yesterday.

10. We often _____ many interesting souvenirs from trips.

Pair Activity

Agree or disagree with your partner's statement.

	Agree	Disagree
Example: I went sightseeing.	So did I.	I didn't.
I didn't go shopping.	Neither did I.	I did.

1. I went to Hong Kong in the summer. (Agree or Disagree)

   _____

   _____

   _____

2. I stayed at a friend's house during my vacation. (Agree or Disagree)

   _____

   _____

   _____

3. I like to go camping. (Agree or Disagree)

   _____

   _____

   _____

4. I took a vacation with my family. (Agree or Disagree)

   _____

   _____

   _____

5. We relaxed at the beach. (Agree or Disagree)

_____

_____

_____

4. I went skiing in the mountain. (Agree or Disagree)

_____

_____

_____

5. I am not going on vacation this year. (Agree or Disagree)

_____

_____

_____

6. I don't like to go shopping. (Agree or Disagree)

_____

_____

_____

7. I can't wait to go on vacation. (Agree or Disagree)

_____

_____

_____

8. I didn't stay in a nice hotel. (Agree or Disagree)

_____

_____

_____

Grammar Practice

Agreeing and Disagreeing in English

One of the easiest ways to agree in English is to say "me too" or "me neither." "Me too" is to agree with a positive statement and "me neither" is to agree with a negative statement. In this case, we do not need to worry about the verb tenses in the responses to the verbs in the original statements. However, when using "so" and "neither" with affirmative and negative statements, we need to consider the verb in the statement and follow the verb in the response. In general, the rule for "So ...... I" and "Neither ...... I" is that the verb agrees with the verb tense used in the original statement.

Always remember to use the verb before the subject.

	Agree	Disagree
I love shopping.	So do I.	I don't.
I was studying yesterday.	So was I.	I wasn't.
I am on vacation.	So am I.	I am not.
I can swim.	So can I.	I can't.
I would like to try it.	So would I.	I wouldn't.
I have visited Asia.	So have I.	I haven't.
I am not working now.	Neither am I.	I am.
I didn't travel this year.	Neither did I.	I did.
I wasn't at the beach.	Neither was I.	I was.
I can't wait to go on vacation.	Neither can I.	I can.

Pointers to Remember

When we talk about taking a vacation, we often mean traveling somewhere. So, when someone says he or she took a vacation, we want to know where the person visited for vacation. Thus, provide pertinent information such as where you have visited and perhaps interesting activities you have done while on the trip when you talk about vacation. We sometimes hear some people say "they took a staycation." "Staycation" is a new word that some people indicate a holiday spent at home.

▌Photo by Link Hoang on Unsplash

Class Activity

What is your dream vacation?

Make a list of places you would like to visit. Share your information with other students and ask them of their dream vacation places.

My Vacation List	Classmate #1	Classmate #2	Classmate #3
1. Paris			
2.			
3.			
4.			

Example: You: I want to visit Paris someday.

Your Classmate: Why Paris?

You: I want to see the Eiffel Tower. It looks so pretty.

How about you? What is your dream vacation?

Photo by David McEachan from Pexels

Special Reading

Where are the most popular cities to visit in the world?

According to the survey done by Mastercard in 2018, Bangkok was selected as the most popular city visited by international travelers. In fact, for three consecutive years, travelers chose Bangkok as the most popular city. The survey indicated that the number of overnight visitors in 2018 was around 20 million. Bangkok is famously known for its amazing food, historical temples, and various types of messages and spas. Two cities that followed Bangkok on the list were London and Paris with overnight visitors of around 19 million and 17 million respectively. Some of the other destinations that made to the list of the most popular cities include Dubai, Singapore, New York, Kuala Lumpur, Tokyo, Istanbul, and Seoul.

Photo by Oleksandr Pidvalnyi from Pexels

Reading Exercise

Read the text again. Write T (True) or F (False) for each statement.

1. _____ New York was selected as the most popular city visited by international travelers.

2. _____ London had 19 million overnight visitors in 2018.

3. _____ The number of overnight visitors in 2018 was around 20 million for Bangkok.

4. _____ Seoul had 17 million overnight visitors in 2018.

5. _____ Paris is known for its amazing food, historical temples, and spas.

Pair Activity

Of the cities presented in the reading, which city would you like to visit the most and why?

_____

_____

_____

_____

_____

_____

_____

Key Expressions to Remember

1. **How was your summer vacation?**

   당신의 여름 방학은 어땠어요?

2. **How was it?**

   어땠어요?

3. **Do you have any plans for the winter?**

   겨울을 위한 계획이 있습니까?

4. **Are you good at skiing?**

   스키 잘 타세요?

5. **What did you do there?**

   거기서 뭐 했어요?

6. **I did sightseeing.**

   관광을 했습니다.

7. **I want to try camping.**

   저는 캠핑을 시도 하고자 합니다.

8. **I want to visit Paris.**

   저는 파리를 방문하고 싶습니다.

9. **So did I.**

   저도 했습니다.

10. **It was amazing.**

    그것은 훌륭했습니다.

Airline Service Expressions

Securing Baggage [짐 보관 안내]

1. **May I help you with your baggage?**
   짐 보관을 도와 드릴까요?

2. **This bin is full. Let me move your bag to another bin with more room.**
   이쪽 선반은 가득 찼습니다. 가방을 더 많은 공간이 있는 다른 선반으로 옮겨 드리겠습니다.

3. **Do you have any valuable item?**
   혹시 귀중품은 없으십니까?

4. **I'm sorry, but you cannot store your baggage here.**
   죄송합니다만 짐은 여기에 보관하실 수 없습니다.

5. **We need to keep the aisle clear.**
   통로에는 짐을 놓으실 수 없습니다.

6. **Would you please store your baggage under the seat in front of you?**
   짐은 앞좌석 아래에 놓아 주십시오.

7. **We do not provide coat check service.**
   의류 보관서비스가 제공되지 않습니다.

8. **Would you please put your coat in the overhead bin?**
   의류 보관은 위쪽 선반에 보관해 주십시오.

9. **You can store your baggage in this overhead bin.**
   이쪽 선반에 짐을 보관하실 수 있습니다.

10. **Please check the baggage to our staff.**
    그 짐은 우리 직원에게 맡겨 주시기 바랍니다.

Practice Your English

A. Speaking Activity 1. What do you like to do on vacation?

Ask 'what do you like to do on vacation?' Use the following activities to respond to the question. Take turns asking and answering the question. Use the present tense verbs.

> Example:
> A: What do you like to do on vacation?
> B: I enjoy trying new food when I am on vacation. How about you?
> A: Me too! I also enjoy relaxing when I am on vacation.

A. fishing

B. shopping

C. sightseeing

D. relaxing

E. rock climbing

F. trying new food

G. hiking

H. scuba diving

I. sailing

J. camping

K. kayaking

L. sun bathing

M. visiting a museum

O. skiing

P. snow boarding

B. Speaking Activity 2. What did you do on vacation?

Ask 'what did you do on vacation?' Use the following activities to respond to the question. Take turns asking and answering the question. Use the past tense verbs.

> **Example:**
> A: What did you do on vacation?
> B: I went hiking when I traveled to Utah. How about you?
> A: Really? I went camping for my last vacation.

A. fishing

B. shopping

C. sightseeing

D. jet skiing

E. rock climbing

F. bike riding

G. hiking

H. scuba diving

I. sailing

J. camping

K. kayaking

L. sun bathing

M. bungee jumping

O. skiing

P. snow boarding

Global English :

Everyday Conversational
English with Airline
Service Talk

Unit
07

Expressing opinions, likes, and dislikes

의견, 좋아하는 것 및 싫어하는 것 표현하기

Expressing opinions, likes, and dislikes
의견, 좋아하는 것 및 싫어하는 것 표현하기

Introduction

During a discussion when you are expressing an opinion. it is important to know how to provide your opinion in a courteous manner. You may agree or disagree with other people's perspectives, but the key is to express your opinion in a polite way. Understanding common English phrases to agree and disagree and to give your personal likes and dislikes will be useful in everyday English conversations as well as in discussions.

▍Photo by rawpixel on Unsplash

Warm Up Activity

What are some ways to agree and to disagree? See the expressions below and indicate "agreeing" or "disagreeing" after each sentence.

Agreeing or Disagreeing

1. I understand your point.   _____

2. I don't share your opinion.   _____

3. I am sorry, but I don't think so.   _____

4. I am sorry, but I think differently.   _____

5. I have the same view.   _____

6. Yes, I know how you feel.   _____

7. I think so too.   _____

8. Sorry, but I don't feel the same.   _____

9. Yes, I don't think so either.   _____

10. I am afraid I don't agree with you.   _____

Conversation 1

Alex: What are you doing this weekend?

Tammy: I am watching a movie with my roommate.

Alex: Really? What kind?

Tammy: I am watching a romantic comedy. Do you want to come?

Alex: That sounds fun, but I prefer watching an action movie.

Tammy: I like watching an action movie, too. But my favorite actress is in the new romantic comedy, so I am excited to watch it. You can come if you like.

Alex: Thanks, but I will pass. Enjoy your weekend though!

 **Conversation 2**

Emma: Do you like living in the city?

Mark: It is not too bad. But I think country life is better.

Emma: Really? I think differently. City life is much better than country life. We have a great public transportation system in the city.

Mark: Yes, I do agree with you on that. But life here in the city is always too busy and it is too crowded. I miss the open space and clean air.

Emma: I can understand how you feel. Sometimes it is nice to get away from the city.

 Speaking Activity

Express Your Opinion. Do you agree or disagree?

Discuss the statements below with your partner and express your opinion.

1. Parents should not allow children to eat fast food.

_____

_____

_____

2. There should be no homework for elementary school students.

_____

_____

_____

3. Healthcare should be free for all citizens.

_____

_____

_____

4. College education should be required for all citizens.

_____

_____

_____

5. Smoking should be banned for all citizens.

_____

_____

_____

6. Exercising is a good habit.

_____

_____

_____

7. Everyone must recycle.

_____

_____

_____

8. It is a good idea to have students wear a school uniform.

_____

_____

_____

9. Celebrities make too much money.

_____

_____

_____

10. Cell phones should not be allowed in the classroom.

_____

_____

_____

What is your opinion? Use the expressions from the warm-up activity to agree or to disagree with your partner's statement.

> **Example:** Your Partner: I think cell phones should not be allowed in the classroom.
>
> You: I don't share your opinion. What if there is an emergency?
>
> If that happens, we should be able to make phone calls.

_____

_____

_____

_____

_____

_____

_____

_____

Grammar Practice

The Simple Present Tense 현재시제

Use the simple present tense verbs when talking about actions in the present that do not usually change. See the following different uses of the present tense:
대개 변경되지 않는 현재의 동작에 대해 이야기 할 때 단순 현재 시제 동사를 사용하라. 현재 시제의 다음과 같은 다양한 용도를 참조하라.

Present Habits	I often exercise on weekends. I usually do not eat breakfast. 현재 습관: 저는 주말에 운동을 자주합니다. 저는 보통 아침 식사를 하지 않습니다.
Opinions and Feelings	I enjoy eating spicy food. My boss does not like drinking coffee. 의견 및 느낌: 저는 매운 음식 먹는 것을 즐깁니다. 저의 사장님은 커피 마시는 것을 좋아하지 않습니다.
General Facts and Truths	Many graduates worry about finding a job after they graduate. 일반적인 사실과 진실: 많은 졸업생들은 졸업 후에 직업을 찾는 것에 대해 걱정합니다.

Comprehension Check Exercise

Read the sentences below. Write H for habits, O for opinions and feelings, and G for general facts and truths.

1. George enjoys watching soccer games.   _____

2. Junk food is bad for your health.   _____

3. Mr. Zach likes Italian food.   _____

4. I exercise every day at the gym.   _____

5. Smoking can cause cancer.   _____

6. I study English every day.   _____

7. I drink coffee every morning.   _____

8. I have three computers at home.   _____

Class Activity

Check out the various types of food below. Go around the class and ask classmates what they like and dislike.

1. pizza

2. hamburger

3. sushi

4. salad

5. dumplings

6. spaghetti

7. kimchi

8. bulgogi

9. steak & cheese sandwich

10. tacos

11. curry rice

12. fish & chips

> **Example:** You: Do you like pizza?
>
> Your partner: Yes, I love pizza. Do you like hamburgers?

Pointers to Remember

Talking about likes and dislikes in a second language classroom is very common. The topic is especially great at the beginning of the class to have students to get to know one another. Remember that there are many other words that are often used interchangeably with the "like" and "dislike" words. Try to use a variety of phrases to get the meaning across.

See the following list for similar words and phrases.

like	dislike
enjoy	don't like
am fond of	am not fond of
love	hate
adore	detest
care for	don't care for

Pair Activity

Ask your partner "do you like.....? or what do you think of...?" questions below. Then write down his/her response in a complete sentence using the third person singular form.

> Example: You: Do you like watching movies?
>
> Your partner: Yes, I love watching movies.
>
> Write: My partner loves watching movies.
>
> You: What do you think of spicy food?
>
> Your partner: I am not too fond of it.
>
> Write: My partner is not fond of spicy food.

1. reading books?

2. going to a live concert?

3. traveling to a foreign country?

4. meeting new people?

5. learning a new language?

6. spicy food?

7. animals?

8. classical music?

9. coffee/tea?

10. cold weather?

_____

_____

_____

_____

_____

_____
_____
_____
_____
_____

🏆 **Class Activity**

What do you and your partner have in common?

Share your information with the class. Write two affirmative statements using "like" and "dislike" words. Try to use other similar words for like and dislike. Have students share their information with the rest of the class.

> **Example:** We both like classical music. We also like coffee. We are not fond of spicy food. We also don't like reading books.

_____
_____
_____
_____
_____
_____
_____
_____
_____
_____

Key Expressions to Remember

1. **Do you like watching movies?**

   영화 보는 것을 좋아합니까?

2. **What do you think about live concerts?**

   라이브 콘서트에 대해 어떻게 생각하세요?

3. **Do you agree?**

   동의합니까?

4. **How do you feel about it?**

   이것에 대해 어떻게 생각하세요?

5. **I understand your point.**

   당신의 관점을 이해합니다.

6. **Sorry, but I think differently.**

   미안하지만, 저는 다르게 생각합니다.

7. **I am afraid I don't agree with you.**

   죄송하지만, 저는 동의하지 않아요.

8. **I am fond of meeting new people.**

   저는 새로운 사람들을 만나는 것을 좋아합니다.

9. **We both enjoy camping.**

   우리는 캠핑을 즐깁니다.

10. **I don't care for cold weather.**

    저는 추운 날씨를 좋아하지 않아요.

Airline Service Expressions

🏷 **Meal Service** [식사 서비스]

1. **We will be serving lunch shortly.**

   곧 점심 식사를 제공 할 것입니다.

2. **May I help you set up your tray table now?**

   지금 트레이 테이블을 세우도록 도와 드릴까요?

3. **I'll ask the passenger in front of you.**

   앞좌석 손님께 협조를 부탁드리겠습니다.

4. **Would you please return your seatback for the passenger behind you?**

   식사하시는 동안 뒤에 계신 손님의 식사를 위해 좌석등받이를 세워 주시겠습니까?

❚ Photo by Suhyeon Choi on Unsplash

5. **What would you like to drink with your meal?**

식사와 함께 음료는 무엇으로 드시겠습니까?

6. **We have three meal options today: beef with vegetables, chicken with rice, and seafood with pasta.**

세 가지 식사 옵션이 있습니다: 야채를 곁들인 소고기 요리, 밥과 닭고기 요리 그리고 파스타를 곁들이 해산물 요리.

7. **I'm sorry. We have run out of beef. How about chicken, instead?**

죄송합니다. 소고기는 모두 서비스 되었습니다. 닭고기 요리는 어떠십니까?

8. **Would you like some wine? We have white wine and red wine.**

와인 드시겠습니까? 화이트 와인과 레드 와인이 있습니다.

9. **Would you like some tea? We have green tea and earl grey tea.**

차 드시겠습니까? 녹차와 얼그레이 차 있습니다.

10. **Are you finished with your meal? May I take it?**

식사 맛있게 드셨습니까? 치워드려도 되겠습니까?

Practice Your English

A. Speaking Activity 1. Complete the survey with information about your partner.

Movie Questionnaire

Questions	Responses
What is your favorite movie genre?	
How often do you watch a movie?	
Who is your favorite actor/actress? Why?	
What is your all time favorite movie? Why	
Where do you watch a movie?	

Example: You: What is your favorite movie genre?

Your Partner: My favorite movie genre is romance.

You: How often do you watch a movie?

Your Partner: I watch it every weekend.

You: What is your all time favorite movie? Why?

Your Partner: My all time favorite movie is Titanic. I liked the story.

You: Where do you watch a move?

Your Partner: I usually watch it at a movie theater.

B. Speaking Activity 2. What is your favorite .... ? Get to know more about your partner.

1. What is your favorite kind of food?
2. What is your favorite travel destination?
3. Who is your favorite movie star?
4. What is your favorite subject?
5. What is your favorite kind of music?
6. What is your favorite movie?
7. What is your favorite thing to do?
8. What is your favorite snack?
9. What is your favorite season?
10. What is your favorite book?

Global English :
Everyday Conversational English with Airline Service Talk

Unit
08

Expressing Preference

우선권에 대해 표현하기

Expressing Preference
우선권에 대해 표현하기

 Introduction

In general, there are different ways we can talk about our tastes or preferences. In this chapter, we will learn various expressions to signal what people generally like or prefer.

 Warm Up Activity

Express your preference using the following expressions.

I prefer	I much prefer ....
I like ..... more than	I much enjoy .... more than ....

1. Dogs vs Cats
2. Watching TV vs Watching movies
3. Listening to music vs Going to the live concert
4. Hamburgers vs Pizza
5. Coffee vs Tea
6. Studying vs Working
7. Sightseeing vs Resting
8. The city vs The country
9. Steak vs Sushi
10. Apples vs Oranges

Example: I prefer dogs. I much prefer dogs. I like dogs more than cats.
I much enjoy playing with dogs more than playing with cats.

_____

_____

_____

_____

_____

_____

_____

_____

_____

_____

_____

_____

_____

 **Conversation 1**

Peter: I am making coffee for myself. Would you like some?

Leslie: I prefer tea over coffee. Do you have some tea instead?

Peter: Sure. What kind of tea do you like? I have green tea and black tea. Which do you prefer?

Leslie: I'd rather have green tea. Thanks.

Peter: No problem. Would you like some milk with it?

Leslie: No, thanks. I prefer my tea plain.

 **Conversation 2**

Rachel: Do you have any plans for the weekend?

Bob: You won't believe it, but I have a blind date.

Rachel: Really? Do you have any idea who you are meeting?

Bob: No, not at all. My friends have set up the blind date.

Rachel: So, what is important to you when you meet someone?

Bob: I like people who are kind and polite.

Rachel: That is all? What else?

Bob: I also like people who are intelligent.

Rachel: Anything else?

Bob: Well, it would be great if the person I am meeting is also attractive.

Rachel: Well, it seems that you have high standards. Good luck with your date!

Pointers to Remember

We generally use words like "prefer" and "like" to express about our preferences. But there are other verbs that we can use to talk about something we like or we prefer.

I enjoy + gerund .... I enjoy swimming.	I much enjoy + gerund .... more than .... I much enjoy reading books more than watching movies.
I am fond of + gerund (or noun).........] I am fond of eating spicy food.	I am fond of + gerund (or noun) .... more than .... I am fond of spicy food more than plain food.
I would rather + verb .... I would rather go out.	I would rather + verb .... more than .... I would rather visit New York more than California.

Photo by rawpixel.com from Pexels

Questions about preferences:

Which do you prefer, coffee or tea?

Which do you enjoy more, soccer or baseball?

Are you fond of swimming or hiking?

Would you rather have lunch or dinner?

Expressing Preferences:

I prefer tea to coffee.

I enjoy soccer more.

I am fond of hiking more. I am fond of cars.

I would rather have lunch with you.

Photo by Plush Design Studio from Pexels

Grammar Practice

Relative Pronouns

Relative pronouns, who, which, and that, are connecting words that help introduce or describe the noun phrase in the independent sentence. 'Who' is used for people, 'which' is used for things, and 'that' is used either for people or things. We use relative pronouns to introduce defining adjective clauses or to connect two independent and dependent sentences. The verb that follows the relative pronoun needs to agree in number with the noun in the main clause.

Example:

I like people **who** are friendly.

I work with a guy **who** has a dog.

I have friends **who** have children.

My brother works at a company **which** sells cell phones.

There are people **that** are very generous.

✎ Comprehension Check Exercise

A. Select the appropriate words in the box to complete the sentences below.

polite	funny	interesting	competent	cars	tasty
spicy	bright	romantic	reliable	kind	loyal

1. I like people who are _____.

2. I ate dinner that was quite _____.

3. My brother works for a company that makes _____.

4. She likes watching movies that are _____.

5. I read a book that is _____.

6. We need to hire someone who is _____.

7. He doesn't like eating food that is _____.

8. I have a car that is _____.

9. A great friend is someone who is _____.

10. I prefer people who are _____.

B. Combine each pair of sentences. Rewrite using who, that, or which.

> Example: I watched a movie. The movie was excellent.
> **I watched a movie which was excellent.**

1. He is a successful person. He works hard for his business.

   _____

   _____

   _____

2. I have a friend. She speaks five languages.

   _____

   _____

   _____

3. I visited a beautiful city. It was in France.

   _____

   _____

   _____

4. I read a book. The book was famous and old.

   _____

   _____

   _____

5. I borrowed a car. The car was fancy and expensive.

   _____

   _____

   _____

6. My boss is workaholic. She is always stressed.

_____

_____

_____

7. I am dating a person. He lives in London.

_____

_____

_____

8. I have been living in New York. New York is a great place for artists.

_____

_____

_____

9. I met a person in San Francisco. She works for a famous tech company.

_____

_____

_____

10. They were successful students. They earned academic scholarships throughout their college years.

_____

_____

_____

Pair Activity

You are looking for a new roommate for your apartment. Write a short paragraph in terms of what characteristics are important in a roommate. Compare your paragraph with a partner.

Example: Hello, my name is Hannah. I am 23 years old and currently studying business major in Seoul. I am looking for a roommate who is similar in age. I am outgoing and sociable, so I enjoy meeting new people. I get along well with people who are both introverted and outgoing. I would like to find a roommate who is organized and clean. It is important that she is a friendly person. Please contact me if you are looking for a place.

You: What is important to you in a roommate?

Your Partner: I want a roommate who is fun. How about you?

You: I would like a roommate who is organized and clean.

_____

_____

_____

_____

_____

_____

_____

_____

Class Activity

You are looking for a new person for the sales department in your company. See the list below and select the qualities that are important to you. Share the qualities to the class.

adaptable - 적응을 잘하는	easygoing - 느긋한, 소탈한
approachable - 친근한	energetic - 활기가 넘치는, 정력적인
ambitious - 야망 있는	enthusiastic/passionate - 열광적인
active - 활동적인	friendly - 친절한, 다정스러운
attentive - 주의를 살피는, 배려하는	flexible - 융통성이 있는
amiable - 정감 있는	independent - 독립적인
calm - 차분한	open-minded- 개방적인, 마음이 열려있는
committed/dedicated - 헌신적인	organized - 정리를 잘하는, 체계적인
compassionate/caring - 인정 많은	polite - 공손한, 정중한
cheerful - 쾌활한, 발랄한	patient - 인내심이 강한
cooperative - 협조적인	reliable/trustworthy - 믿을 수 있는
creative/imaginative - 창의력이 있는	thoughtful/understanding - 배려 깊은
diligent/hardworking - 성실한, 근면한	sociable/outgoing - 사교 적인, 외향적인
determined - 결심이 많은	warm-hearted - 마음이 따듯한
sensible - 똑똑한	decisive - 결단력이 있는
sincere - 성실한	witty/resourceful/clever - 재치 있는
confident - 자신감 있는	perceptive - 지각 있는
generous - 후한, 아량이 넓은	punctual - 시간을 잘 지키는
devoted - 헌신적인	bright - 똑똑한
humorous - 재미있는	insightful - 통찰력 있는
responsible - 책임감이 강한	positive - 긍정적인

Example: It is important that people are diligent and polite. I also like people who are friendly.

Special Reading

What are your favorite in-flight snacks?

While many domestic airlines provide in-flight snacks for a fee, most airlines provide complimentary in-flight snacks for their international travelers during long flights. Latnam Airline in Latin America offers one of the tastiest in-flight snacks. The airline offers only one kind of snack, which is called Alfajores cookies, made out of almond cookies dipped in either milk or white chocolate. Unlike Latnam Airline, Korean Air provides a variety of snack options to its international travelers. These snacks include pizza, hot bun with seasoned meat, cookies, brownies, shrimp prawn crackers, and samgak kimbap which is triangle rice cake covered with dried seaweed. Not all international flights have these snacks at the same time, but the Korean Air passengers can experience some of these snacks on their international flights and many of them can ask for more than one snack.

Delta Airline in America also offers complimentary several snack options for its domestic and international airline passengers. These in-flight snacks are those famous Biscoff cookies, pretzels, roasted peanuts, and yogurt granola bars. Some of the other airlines' famous snacks include Air France's fresh stuffed croissant or sandwich, Turkish Airline's Turkish delight, and Hawaiian Airline's furikake chips (made from sweet potatoes & taro) and ranch tasting popcorn. While most travelers do not choose airlines solely based on snack options, these tasty snacks will certainly help traveling more enjoyable.

Reading Exercise

Read the text again. Answer the questions.

1. What are Alfajores cookies?

_____

_____

2. What kind of snacks does Korean Air provide for their international travelers?

_____

_____

3. Who offers Biscoff cookes, pretzels, and roasted peanuts?

_____

_____

Photo by Jade Wulfraat on Unsplash

Key Expressions to Remember

1. **Do you prefer coffee or tea?**

   커피와 차 중 어떤 걸 드시겠어요?

2. **Which do you prefer?**

   어느 쪽을 선호합니까?

3. **What kind of tea do you like?**

   어떤 차의 종류를 좋아합니까?

4. **What do you enjoy more, watching movies or reading books?**

   영화 보는 것과 독서 중 무엇을 더 좋아합니까?

5. **What is important to you?**

   당신에게 중요한 것은 무엇입니까?

6. **I prefer coffee.**

   저는 커피를 더 좋아합니다.

7. **I like people who are kind.**

   저는 친절한 사람들을 좋아합니다.

8. **I would rather have dinner.**

   차라리 저녁을 먹고 싶습니다.

9. **I like dogs more than cats.**

   저는 고양이보다 개를 더 좋아합니다.

10. **What else?**

    그 밖의 무엇을 드릴까요?

Airline Service Expressions

Snack Service in the Plane [기내 스낵 서비스]

1. **Would you care for a snack?**

   스낵 드시겠습니까?

2. **We have chocolate chip cookies, pizza, and plain crackers.**

   스낵은 초콜릿 칩 쿠키, 피자, 일반 크래커가 있습니다.

3. **Which one would you like?**

   무엇으로 드시겠습니까?

4. **This is a hot pie. It has shrimp in it.**

   이것은 뜨거운 파이입니다. 안에 새우가 들어 있습니다.

5. **I'm sorry, but personal food items are not allowed to consume on board.**

   죄송합니다만, 개인 휴대 음식은 기내에서 취식이 불가합니다.

6. **We have spicy Korean instant noodles. Would you like to try?**

   한국 라면이 있습니다. 준비해 드릴까요?

7. **Would you please wait for a moment?**

   잠시만 기다려 주시겠습니까?

8. **It's hot, please be careful.**

   뜨겁습니다. 조심하십시오.

9. **Would you like something to drink?**

   음료 한 잔 드시겠습니까?

10. **Can I get you anything else?**

    더 필요한 것은 없으십니까?

Practice Your English

 Speaking Activity 1

Who are your favorite actors or actresses? What do you like about them? Please share some of the qualities of your favor actors or actresses with a partner.

> **Example:** I like Jennifer Lawrence and Emma Stone. They are beautiful and talented.

_____

_____

_____

_____

_____

 Speaking Activity 2

What kind of .... do you like? Use the expressions from the box to ask your partner of his/her preference. Take turns asking and responding to preference questions.

What kind of movies do you like?

What kind of books do you like?

What kind of music do you like?

What kind of sports do you like?

What kind of TV programs do you like?

What kind of food do you like?

What kind of tea do you like?

I prefer	I much prefer ....
I like ..... more than	I much enjoy .... more than ....

Example: You: What kind of movies do you like?

Your Partner: I prefer romantic comedies. I like to laugh.

Photo by Pietro Jeng from Pexels

Global English:

**Everyday Conversational
English with Airline
Service Talk**

Unit
0 9

Providing suggestions and recommendations

제안 및 권장사항 제공하기

Providing suggestions and recommendations
제안 및 권장사항 제공하기

 Introduction

People usually provide advice when someone they know is in trouble or ask for advice when they are in need of help. In English, there are several verbs and phrases that are often used when providing advice and asking for advice. Depending on the degree of the issue, some verbs and phrases work more appropriately when giving and asking for advice. The goal of this unit is to present key expressions when providing suggestions and recommendations.

🎬 Warm Up Activity

We use modal verbs such as 'should', 'should not', 'have to', and 'don't have to' to provide advice. See each of the advice below and fill in the blank using one of the modal verbs.

1. I am sorry to hear that you are sick. You _____ see a doctor.

2. I _____ eat too much junk food. But they are so delicious.

3. I have a job interview in the early in the morning. I _____
   wake up early.

4. We are all set for the party. You _____ bring anything.

5. You have a big exam tomorrow. You _____ get a good night sleep.

💬 Conversation 1

Andy: Hi, Carol. I am having some problems with my neighbor, and I don't know what to do.

Carol: Oh, really? What is going on?

Andy: My neighbor always has friends over at night, and they often turn on loud music until 2 am in the morning. And this often happens during the weekdays!

Carol: That is terrible! And don't you have classes in the morning?

Andy: Yes! I am always tired in the morning because I can't go to sleep at night.

Carol: I think you should see your apartment manager right away and tell him or her about the issue. The manager has to solve the problem right away because this probably is bothering other neighbors too.

Andy: Good idea. I was going to talk to my neighbor today, but talking to the manager will be more effective.

 **Conversation 2**

Megan: What should we eat today for lunch? I am craving for fried chicken and french fries.

Amy: We had hamburgers and french fries yesterday. How about soup and salad for lunch today?

Megan: You know I don't eat vegetables. Let's eat fried chicken instead.

Amy: You really should eat more vegetables. Eating too much greasy food can make you gain weight and make you have health problems.

Megan: I know you are right, Amy. But it is so difficult to give up on fast food.

Amy: We have to start eating more healthy, Megan. So, how about soup and salad today?

Megan: That is probably a good idea.

Photo by Robin Stickel on Unsplash

Comprehension Check Exercise A

Read the problems in the box. Write advice for each problem. Share the advice with your partner. Does your partner have the same or different advice?

Problem
1. My brother loves eating unhealthy food. I see him ordering pizza or chicken whenever mom and dad are out. He has already gained a lot of weight. But I am worried that he will be unhealthy as a result of his eating habits.
2. My sister is addicted to her cell phone. She is always online browsing the web and playing online games. She rarely goes out because she would rather play with her phone. She sometimes stays up all night playing online games. My family and I are very concerned for her well being, but we don't know how to make her stop.
3. I think my friend is addicted to exercising. Exercising is a good habit, but he complains about his joint pain everyday due to too much exercising.
4. I am so forgetful these days. In the past, I have lost my homework, wallet, and even a cell phone. I am worried that I will miss very important deadlines that will have big consequences.
5. My roommate is a couch potato. She never does anything after work. She watches TV all day long. She never gets up to do any of the house chores. She eats and rests in front of the TV all day and all night long. Dishes and laundry clothes are always piled on high when I come home.
6. My friend is a shopaholic. She spends all her time browsing the web and buying unnecessary items. Many times she doesn't even use the items she buys online. I know she does not have a lot of money, so I am worried that she is charging everything on her credit card. When I visit her house, I see many unopened boxes.

Solution

1.

2.

3.

4.

5.

6.

Pointers to Remember

When we give advice, we often use the modal verbs such as 'should' or 'ought to'. However, when we want to provide stronger advice, we use 'have to', 'had better', or 'must'.

Stronger advice

You <u>have to</u> eat healthy.

Weaker advice

You <u>should</u> eat more vegetables.

Stronger negative advice

You <u>(had) better</u> not eat so much fast food.

Weaker negative advice

You <u>don't</u> have to come to the class tomorrow.

Courtesy of Iclickart

Grammar Practice

Modal Verbs (Giving Advice): Should, ought to, and had better

In English, we use the modal verbs 'should', 'ought to', and 'had better' to give advice and to make suggestions. 'Should' is the most common way to give advice, but it is also considered as not strong advice as 'had better'. When we want to provide strong advice, it is more common to use 'had better' or 'had better not'.

Affirmative Statements

Subject	Modal Verb	Base Form of Verb	
I/You	should	eat	more vegetables.
He/She	ought to	eat	more vegetables.
We/They	had better	eat	more vegetable.

Negative Statements

Subject	Modal Verb	Base Form of Verb	
I/You	should not	eat	fast food.
He/She	ought not to	eat	fast food.
We/They	had better not	eat	fast food.

✒ Comprehension Check Exercise B

Complete the sentences with should, shouldn't, ought to, ought not to, had better, or had better not. Use the appropriate verbs from the box.

eat	spend	meet	avoid	drive
take	send	tell	see	read

1. I think something is wrong with the car. You _____ it to the auto shop.

2. What is wrong? Are you sick? Perhaps you _____ a doctor.

3. It is snowing really hard today. You _____ today.

4. The deadline for the job application is today. You _____ it now.

5. You know eating unhealthy food can make you have lots of health problems. You _____ that fried chicken.

6. We need to start saving money. We _____ less money on un-necessary items.

7. Let's meet for lunch tomorrow. _____ we _____ at the John's Cafe?

8. You _____ this book. It wasn't very interesting.

9. The class is cancelled today. We _____ our classmates.

10. If you are trying to lose weight, you _____ soda.

Pair Activity

What kind of advice would you provide? See the each problem below and take turns giving and receiving advice.

> **Example:** You: My cell phone is too slow. It takes too long to access any
> online information.
> Me: How much data does your phone have? Perhaps you
> should increase data on your phone.

1. My best friend can't keep a secret.

_____

_____

_____

2. My brother is always stressed out. He can't relax.

_____

_____

_____

3. I can't say no to my friends when they ask me for favors.

_____

_____

_____

4. I don't like my coworkers.

_____

_____

_____

5. My car is new, but it is already having problems.

_____

_____

_____

6. My boyfriend is a couch potato. We never do anything.

_____

_____

_____

7. I am so shy. It is difficult for me to make friends.

_____

_____

_____

8. I don't know how to manage my time. I am always late.

_____

_____

_____

9. I don't ever exercise. I am gaining weight.

_____

_____

_____

10. Idea of your own. _____

_____

_____

_____

Special Reading

What are some ways to manage stress?

Everyone gets stressed out at one point or another. However, some people are better at managing their stress. According to some experts, there are ways to handle stress more effectively. One way is to identify the source of the stress and figure out if this stress is something you have control over it. For example, find out if you are always stressed because you have too much work and not enough time to complete it or perhaps you are stressed because you do not know how to manage time more efficiently. Without truly understanding the real source of the stress, it will be difficult to find a solution that works.

Another technique to handle stress is to avoid the stressful situation. So, if a person or an environment is causing you to feel stressed out, limit your encounter with the person. Ideally, it will be nice to communicate with the stressor respectively to solve the issue together. However, if this is not possible, why not change your attitude and perceive the situation in a more positive way? It is important to tell yourself that no stress is more important than you and your health. One of the best ways to reduce stress is to exercise regularly. Experts say that exercise helps to produce endorphins or "feel good" chemicals in the brain to make people feel happy afterward. There are lots of different exercises. Why not try one to help you lower your stress and to help you forget about your stress at least for temporarily? There will always be stressful events, but it is good to know that there are ways to manage stress.

Reading Exercise

Read the text again. Answer the questions.

1. What is one way to manage stress more effectively?

   _____

   _____

2. How does exercise help reduce stress?

   _____

   _____

3. What are endorphins?

   _____

   _____

Key Expressions to Remember

1. **What is going on?**

   무슨 일입니까?

2. **What should we have for lunch?**

   점심 식사를 무엇을 먹을까요?

3. **How about soup and salad?**

   수프와 샐러드 어떻습니까?

4. **What should I do?**

   제가 어떻게 해야 할까요?

5. **I am worried about him.**

   그분이 걱정이 되요.

6. **You have to eat healthy food.**

   건강에 좋은 음식을 먹어야 합니다.

7. **You ought to eat more vegetables.**

   당신은 더 많은 채소를 먹어야 합니다.

8. **You had better not eat fast food anymore.**

   더 이상 패스트푸드를 먹지 않는 것이 좋습니다.

9. **You should not drink soda.**

   탄산 음료수를 마시지 않는 것이 좋습니다.

10. **I eat too much junk food.**

    저는 너무 많은 정크 푸드를 먹어요.

Airline Service Expressions

Helping Sick Passengers [아픈 승객 안내]

1. Can I help you?

무엇을 도와드릴까요?

2. Do you have any additional blanket?

담요가 더 있습니까?

3. I'll check if there is any additional blanket.

담요가 더 있는지 확인해 드리겠습니다.

4. I'll bring it for you right away.

곧 가져다 드리겠습니다.

Photo by Steven Thompson on Unsplash

5. Excuse me, do you have anything for a headache?

실례합니다, 두통약이 있습니까?

6. Yes, we have Tylenol on board.

예, 기내에 타이레놀을 가지고 있습니다.

7. Do you have any allergies to any medicine?

약 알레르기가 있습니까?

8. Would you like one or two tablets?

하나 또는 두 개의 약을 드시겠습니까?

9. I will check the cabin temperature.

기내 온도를 확인해 보겠습니다.

10. Would you like a hot drink?

따뜻한 음료는 어떠십니까?

Practice Your English

A. Listening / Speaking / Reading / Writing Activity. Read the following letter to Abigail. Then discuss the issues in the letter. Work together to compose advice for the person in the letter.

January 25th

Dear Abigail,

My family and I took a trip to Europe for about 10 days during our winter vacation. It was a great trip, and we all had a lot of fun. At the time when we were traveling, we stayed at a nice hotel, ate at famous restaurants, and bought interesting souvenirs. Now that we are back from the trip, I finally figured out how much money we had spent during our trip. We definitely spent more than our means. I haven't told my wife, but I know she will get upset. Our children's birthdays are coming up next month, but it will be difficult to give them a party or any presents. I don't know what to do.

Sincerely,

Worried Father

Advice

_____

_____

_____

_____

_____

Global English:

Everyday Conversational
English with Airline
Service Talk

Unit
10

Talking about past events

과거의 사건들에 대해 이야기하기

Talking about past events
과거의 사건들에 대해 이야기하기

 Introduction

Learning about the simple past tense verbs can be straightforward after understanding the simple present tense verbs. We use the simple past tense to show an action that was completed in the past. The rule is to add an -ed suffix for regular verbs. However, for beginning second language students, it is difficult to know which verb is regular or irregular. For irregular verbs, the rule of adding an -ed suffix doesn't apply. By introducing regular and irregular past tense verbs in this unit, students will have opportunities to learn and to practice using them in a meaningful way.

Warm Up Activity

We often use time expressions to help us differentiate habitual present events from finished past time events. See the time expressions below and indicate a present event or a past event after each time expression.

Example: last week	past event
	present/past

1. every year _____

2. last week _____

3. each night _____

4. once a month _____

5. three days ago _____

6. when + finished event _____

7. last Monday _____

 **Conversation 1**

Danny: Hi Sarah! How was your weekend?

Sarah: It was great. I went camping with some friends.

Danny: Really? What did you do there?

Sarah: We went hiking and cooked some outdoor meals.

Danny: Wow. That sounds a lot of fun. Wasn't it chilly at night?

Sarah: Yes! How did you know?

Danny: I went camping last year around this time of a year, and I remember the weather was pretty cold.

Sarah: It did get a bit cold at night, so we made a campfire and cooked some marshmallows.

Danny: So did we! I want to go camping again.

Sarah: Let's try to go together next time.

 **Conversation 2**

John: Did you participate in the outdoor activity last week?

Harry: Yes, we visited a local art museum. Why didn't you come?

John: I couldn't. I was sick. How was the museum?

Harry: Sorry to hear that. The museum was interesting. There were lots of beautiful paintings. Are you feeling better?

John: Not really. Because I was sick last week, I didn't finish my class project. Did you finish yours?

Harry: Yes. I finished it last week and turned it in already.

John: Was the project due last week?

Harry: I believe so. Perhaps you could turn it in today since you were sick. Get
better soon.

Comprehension Check Exercise A

Read the conversations 1 and 2 again and underline all the past tense verbs.
Create new sentences with those past tense verbs.

1. _____

2. _____

3. _____

4. _____

5. _____

6. _____

7. _____

8. _____

9. _____

10. _____

Pointers to Remember

When talking about your travel experience, indicate where/when you have visited and for how long you have visited the place. You can also talk about the fun activities you have done and the memorable moments of your trip. Use the following questions to help you talk about your own travel experience.

1. Where did you go on vacation?

2. When did you go on vacation?

3. Who did you go with?

4. What did you do there?

5. How did you like it?

6. What was the most memorable moment of your trip?

7. Did you enjoy the trip?

8. Would you like to visit the place again?

Photo by rawpixel.com from Pexels

Grammar Practice

The Simple Past Tense: Past Events

When talking about actions completed in the past, we use the simple past tense verbs. For regular verbs, we simply add -ed or -d to the present tense form of the verb. For example, for a verb 'learn', we add -ed by making the present tense verb 'learn' into the past tense verb 'learned.' However, for irregular verbs, the rule doesn't apply. See Appendix 4 for irregular verbs.

Affirmative Statements	Negative Statements
He **worked** at a bakery.	He **did not work** at a bakery.
My teacher **liked** fast food.	My teacher **didn't like** fast food.
My sister **watched** a lot of movies.	My sister **didn't watch** a lot of movies.
She **studied** a lot every day.	She **didn't study** a lot every day.
My brother **tried** to exercise twice a week.	My brother **didn't try** to exercise twice a week.

See the spelling rules in the simple past tense.

Regular Verb	Spelling Rule
work (a consonant) want	Add -ed worked / wanted
enjoy (a vowel + y) play	Add -ed enjoyed / played
study (a consonant + y) try	Change -y to -i, add -ed studied / tried
like (a consonant + e) bike	Add -d liked / biked
stop (consonant + vowel + consonant) drop	Double the consonant, add -ed stopped / dropped

✏ Comprehension Check Exercise B

Complete the sentences using the simple past.

1. I missed the bus, so I _____ (walk) to school today.

2. I _____ (sleep) early last night, so I am not tired this morning.

3. My mother _____ (drive) me to school since I woke up late.

4. My teacher _____ (want) to buy additional pencils for her students.

5. They _____ (like) the movie but didn't like the actors in it.

6. My sister _____ (graduate) this year with a nursing degree.

7. My family and I _____ (visit) the Statue of Liberty in New York.

8. Last summer I _____ (work) at a family restaurant as a waitress for about 2 months.

Pair Activity

Where did you go on vacation? Take turns asking and telling about your most recent vacation trip. Use the questions below to start the conversation.

1. Where did you go on vacation?

2. When did you go on vacation?

3. Who did you go with?

4. What did you do there?

5. How did you like it?

6. What was the most memorable moment of your trip?

7. Did you enjoy the trip?

8. Would you like to visit the place again?

_____

_____

_____

_____

_____

_____

_____

_____

_____

_____

_____

_____

Class Activity

Fun Speaking Game: Who is telling the truth?

Write two true statements about yourself that happened in the past. Give the statements to the group leader or the instructor. You need to include your name with your statements.

The group leader chooses one person's statement. Have the person who wrote the statement and two other people come to the front of the class. Write the statement on the board. Have the class ask questions to the three selected students to find out who is telling the truth. Selected students should act to make the class believe the chosen statement is their statement.

> **Example:** I visited Spain with my family when I was in high school.

The class asks each person questions: How long did you stay in Spain? Where did you stay? What did you do there? What did you eat there?

The job of the class is to ask each person a variety of questions to figure out who is really telling the truth.

Write Two Statements About Yourself.

_____

_____

_____

_____

_____

_____

Key Expressions to Remember

1. **How was your weekend?**

   주말 어떻게 보내셨어요?

2. **What did you do there?**

   거기서 뭐 했어요?

3. **How did you like it?**

   그거 어땠어요?

4. **Did you enjoy the trip?**

   그 여행을 즐기셨어요?

5. **We went camping.**

   우리는 캠핑을 갔다 왔어요.

6. **I visited New York last year.**

   작년에 뉴욕을 방문했습니다.

7. **We liked the trip.**

   우리는 그 여행을 좋아했어요.

8. **I did not like the food.**

   저는 그 음식을 좋아하지 않았습니다.

9. **I worked at a cafe.**

   저는 카페에서 일했습니다.

10. **I studied music.**

    저는 음악을 공부했습니다.

Photo by Gus Ruballo on Unsplash

Airline Service Expressions

Selling Duty-Free Items [면세품]

1. We are selling duty-free items.

   면세품 판매하고 있습니다.

2. Would you like to buy any duty-free item?

   면세품을 구매하시겠습니까?

3. Please see the in-flight catalog in front of your seat pocket.

   좌석 주머니에 있는 잡지를 참고해 주십시오.

4. The duty-free allowance is three bottles.

   면세기준은 술 세 병입니다.

5. How would you like to pay?

지불은 어떻게 하시겠습니까?

6. The exchange rate in the cabin is 1,170 won to the dollar.

기내 환율은 달러당 1,170원입니다.

7. Do you have any other currency, instead?

대신 다른 화폐는 없으십니까?

8. We take Korean Won, US Dollar, Japanese Yen and Chinese Yuan.

사용 가능한 화폐는 한국 원, 미국 달러, 일본 엔, 중국 위안화입니다.

9. You can pay by cash and credit card together.

카드와 현금을 같이 결제하실 수 있습니다.

10. We accept all major credit cards.

저희는 모든 주요 신용 카드를 받습니다.

Special Reading

Where are the biggest duty-free airports in the world?

When international travelers travel around the world, many of them make a point to shop at a duty-free store. A duty-free shop is a retail store that sells luxury and lower end goods without certain local or national taxes. This incentive makes shopping more enjoyable and enticing for travelers. While all of the international airports have many duty free retailers, there are some airports that are more famously known as the major duty-free airports in the world.

The first one on the list is Dubai International Airport, which is the busiest airport in the world, has the biggest duty-free retailers in the world. Following the Dubai International Airport, London's Heathrow Airport is considered as one of the largest duty-free airports in Europe because of its size. Hong Kong International and the Paris Charles de Gaulle Airport in France respectively come into third and fourth as the top duty-free airports. The last one on the list is Seoul Incheon International Airport in South Korea, which has over 90 duty-free retailers.

Reading Exercise

Read the text again. Answer the questions.

1. Why do many international travelers shop at duty-free stores?

   _____

   _____

   _____

2. Which airport has the biggest duty-free retailers in the world?

   _____

   _____

   _____

3. Which airport has over 90 duty-free retailers?

   _____

   _____

   _____

4. What do you usually buy at the duty-free stores?

   _____

   _____

   _____

5. Have you been to any of the top duty-free airports mentioned in the reading?

   _____

   _____

   _____

Practice Your English

A. Writing / Speaking Activity. Write a letter to your friend about a recent trip you took. Talk about the place you visited and any fun moments of the trip. Share the letter with your partner.

_____

_____

_____

_____

_____

_____

B. Speaking Activity. Think about what you did last weekend. Share the information with you partner. Take turns asking and telling your weekend story. Make sure to keep the conversation going by asking questions and providing reactions.

> **Example:** Student A: I saw a movie last weekend.
>
> Student B: Really? What did you watch?
>
> Student A: I watched _____.
>
> Student B: Nice! Was it good?

_____

_____

_____

_____

Global English :

Everyday Conversational English with Airline Service Talk

Unit
11

Talking about
personal experiences

개인적인 경험에 대해 말하기

Talking about personal experiences
개인적인 경험에 대해 말하기

Introduction

When talking about personal events or experiences that took place in the past, it can be difficult for second language students to know whether to use past tense or present perfect tense verbs. In this unit, students will differentiate the past simple from the present perfect and practice using the present perfect in a meaningful way.

Warm Up Activity

The present perfect tense refers to a time prior to now but is still relevant in the present. We use have/has + past participle to form a sentence. Please rewrite the following past tense sentences by making them into present perfect tense sentences.

> **Example:** I ate Mexican food. → I have eaten Mexican food.

1. I rode a horse.

_____

_____

_____

2. My brother worked in the engineering field.

_____

_____

3. My sister traveled to France.

_____

_____

4. I did not work at a cafe.

_____

_____

5. I tried bungee jumping.

_____

_____

▌Photo from pixabay.com

 **Conversation 1**

Erica: What is your favorite food, Amy?

Amy: I like all kinds of food. But I would say my favorite food is Pad Thai. Have you tried it?

Erica: No, I haven't. What is it?

Amy: Pad Thai is a famous Thai dish made with wide noodles, bean sprouts, onion, egg, and finely ground peanuts. I am surprised you haven't tried it.

Erica: It sounds delicious, but I am allergic to peanuts. So that is probably why I have never eaten it.

Amy: I see. I am pretty adventurous with food. Have you ever tried Indian food? I hear there is a new Indian restaurant at the mall.

Erica: Yes, I have. I like Indian food. Let's go there this weekend.

 **Conversation 2**

Interviewer: Have you worked as a flight attendant before?

Interviewee: No, I haven't. But I have a degree in airline service, and I have various work experiences in the service industry.

Interviewer: Where have you worked?

Interviewee: I have worked in a family restaurant and a cafe. At the moment, I work for a marketing company in the customer service department.

Interviewer: How long have you been working there?

Interviewee: Since last summer, so, for about a year now.

Interviewer: What have you learned from working in the service industry so far?

Interviewee: From working in the service industry, I have gained excellent communication and service skills. Being in the service industry, I work with a variety of people. So, I have become confident serving the needs of various customers.

Comprehension Check Exercise A

Please answer the questions from the conversations. Use complete sentences.

1. From the conversation 1, has Erica tried Indian food?

_____

2. Why hasn't Erica ever tried Pad Thai before?

_____

3. What is Pad Thai?

_____

4. In conversation 2, where has the interviewee worked before?

_____

5. In conversation 2, how long has the interviewee worked for the marketing company?

_____

6. Has the interviewee worked as a flight attendant before?

_____

7. Do you think the interviewee is suitable for the cabin crew position?

_____

Speaking Activity

Walk around the classroom and find someone who has done each of the activities below. Try to maintain the conversation by using conversational techniques, such as asking follow-up questions and showing reactions.

> **Example:** eat Indian food
>
> Student A: Have you ever eaten Indian food?
>
> Student B: Sure, I have. I really enjoy Indian food. How about you?
>
> Student A: Indian food is one of my favorites. Where do you usually eat Indian food?
>
> Student B: Really? I usually go to the one near the school.

1. travel abroad

2. break a bone

3. have a surgery

4. meet a famous person

5. try bungee jumping

6. fall in love

7. write a book

8. win an award

9. drive a car

10. lose your wallet

Pointers to Remember

We often use time words that indicate the present or the recent past such as <u>just</u>, <u>recently</u>, <u>before</u>, <u>ever</u>, <u>so far</u>, <u>until now</u>, <u>up to now</u>, <u>yet</u>, <u>always</u>, and <u>never</u> with the present perfect.

> Example: Have you always lived here?
>
> What have you been up to now?
>
> Have you finished your project yet?
>
> So far, I have only finished the first part.

However, we do not use time words that indicate the past time such as yesterday, last week, or last year with the present perfect.

> Example: I have seen the movie (yesterday). (WRONG!)
>
> I have bought a new car (last week). (WRONG!)

Grammar Practice

The Present Perfect

Past to Present

We use the present perfect to talk about an event or an action that started in the past and continues in the present.

> **Example:** I have lived in Paris all my life. I have used this piano since I was young.

Life Experience

We use the present perfect to talk about our life experience that happened in the past and is still relevant in the present.

> **Example:** I have visited many countries in Asia. I have worked as a nurse for about 10 years.

Recent Event

We use the present perfect to talk about a recent event or updated news.

> **Example:** I have found a new job. We have discovered a new cure for the disease.

Affirmative Statements	Negative Statements
He **has worked** at a bakery.	He has not **(hasn't) worked** at a bakery.
My teacher **has bought** a new car.	My teacher **hasn't bought** a new car.
My sister **has watched** a lot of movies.	My sister **hasn't watched** a lot of movies.
She **has studied** in Europe.	She **hasn't studied** in Europe.
My brother **has tried** kickboxing.	My brother **hasn't tried** kickboxing.

Comprehension Check Exercise B

Read the sentences below. Select either the past simple or present perfect verb for each sentence.

1. I _____ my favorite wallet last week, so I bought a new one. (lose)

2. My sister _____ New York twice. (visit)

3. I _____ at this company for over a year. (work)

4. I _____ a new job! I start this week. (find)

5. My family and I _____ to Canada last year. (go)

6. Julien _____ me for three years now. (know)

7. Katlin _____ tennis since she was 10 years old. (play)

8. I _____ the bus this morning, so I was late for the meeting. (miss)

9. I _____ the book you gave me! It was so good. (finish)

10. I _____ in California when I was young. (live)

Pair Activity

What interesting things have you done? See the list below and take turns asking and answering questions.

> **Example:** Student A: Have you ever gone skydiving?
>
> Student B: No, I haven't. Have you?
>
> Student A: Yes, I have. I went skydiving this summer.

a. skydiving

b. hang-gliding

c. scuba diving

d. zip-lining

e. snow boarding

f. rock climbing

g. camping

h. water rafting

i. hunting

j. jet skiing

_____

_____

_____

_____

_____

_____

_____

_____

_____

_____

_____

Key Expressions to Remember

1. **What is your favorite food?**

   가장 좋아하는 음식은 무엇입니까?

2. **Have you tried Indian food?**

   인도 음식을 먹어 본 적이 있습니까?

3. **Have you worked there before?**

   전에 거기에서 일 해보셨나요?

4. **Have you ever traveled abroad?**

   해외로 여행 한 적이 있습니까?

5. **How long have you worked there?**

   그곳에서 일한 지 얼마나 되었습니까?

6. **Where have you worked?**

   어디에서 일 해보셨나요?

7. **No, I have never tried Indian food.**

   아니요, 저는 인도 음식을 한번도 시도한 적이 없어요.

8. **I really enjoy the Korean food.**

   저는 한국 음식을 정말로 즐깁니다.

9. **I want to try camping.**

   저는 캠핑을 가고 싶습니다.

10. **So far so good.**

    지금까지 좋은 것 같아요.

Airline Service Expressions

Beverage Service [음료 서비스]

1. **Would you like something to drink?**

   음료 한 잔 드릴까요?

2. **Would you like ice with your drink?**

   얼음과 함께 드시겠습니까?

3. **May I open your tray table?**

   트레이 테이블을 열어도 될까요?

4. **We offer juice, soft drink, wine, beer and so on.**

   주스, 탄산음료, 와인, 맥주 등이 제공되고 있습니다.

Photo by Gus Ruballo on Unsplash

5. **What kind of drink would you like?**

어떤 음료로 드시겠습니까?

6. **Here is your apple juice.**

말씀하신 사과 주스입니다.

7. **Which one would you like?**

무엇으로 드시겠습니까?

8. **Please enjoy your drink.**

맛있게 드십시오.

9. **Would you like some more tea?**

홍차 더 드시겠습니까?

10. **May I take your cup if you are finished?**

다 드셨으면 컵을 치워드려도 되겠습니까?

Practice Your English

A. Writing/Speaking Activity. Write a short paragraph about an interesting experience you have had. This experience can be about meeting someone famous or traveling somewhere fun. Share your experience with your partner. Take turns asking and answering questions.

> **Example:** I met the president of Costa Rica before. In fact, I had lunch
> with him, and I didn't know he was the president of Costa Rica.
> It was an interesting experience.
>
> **Questions:** When did you meet him? How did you meet him? How was
> he? What did you say? What did he say?

B. Speaking Activity. Get to know your classmates. Ask the following survey questions to classmates.

Yes/No	Name	Have you ever ......?	Extra Information
		traveled abroad?	
		failed a test?	
		missed a plane/train/bus?	
		won a lottery?	
		taken singing lessons?	
		felt lonely?	
		seen a celebrity?	
		liked your classmate?	

Share the story with the class.

What was the most interesting story?

What did you learn about your classmates?

Who did you talk to the most?

What was surprising?

_____

_____

_____

_____

_____

_____

_____

_____

_____

_____

Global English:

Everyday Conversational English with Airline Service Talk

Unit
12

Talking about future events

미래의 사건에 대해 말하기

Talking about future events
미래의 사건에 대해 말하기

 Introduction

Deciding whether to use 'will + base verb' or 'be going to + base verb' is natural for native English speakers. However, for second language learning students, it can be a bit challenging. What is the difference between the two forms? Which one is more appropriate to use? In this unit, students will have opportunities to learn different forms of simple future tense and to use them to talk about different aspects of their future plans.

❙ Photo by rawpixel.com from Pexels

Warm Up Activity

We generally use 'going to + base verb' when something is planned for while 'will + base verb' is used when we want to make a promise or make a prediction of a future event. Write a planned action or a promise/prediction next to each sentence.

1. I think it will rain tomorrow. _____

2. My sister is going to college starting this year. _____

3. Promising future doctors will find a cure for cancer. _____

4. My neighbor is a great singer. He will become a famous singer.

   _____

5. I am going to visit Spain next year. _____

6. My roommate is going to cook pasta for dinner tonight.

   _____

7. I am studying so hard tonight, so I will get an A on the test.

   _____

8. I saw the weather forecast for tomorrow. It is going to snow.

   _____

9. I will buy a new computer in the future. _____

10. I will marry someday. _____

 **Conversation 1**

Benjamin: Hi, Nicole! Next week is our spring break. What are you going to do?

Nicole: Hey, Ben. I am planning to visit my sister in California.

Benjamin: Really? I didn't know your sister lived in California. What are you guys planning to do?

Nicole: We really don't know yet. But we will probably go to the beach and maybe go to the Disneyland.

Benjamin: Nice! Will you be driving or riding a plane?

Nicole: I am planning to drive there. It is about a 7 hour drive. What will you do, Ben?

Benjamin: 7 hour drive isn't too bad. I don't have any plans yet, but I am thinking about just relaxing.

Nicole: Sometimes it is nice to just relax. I will probably do that when I get back from California.

Conversation 2

Minjung: Hi, Tim. Are you planning to come to Jina's birthday party tomorrow?

Tim: Jina's party is tomorrow? What time is the party?

Minjung: It is at 6 p.m. Will you come?

Tim: Well, I am going to Jina's party at 6. But I will probably leave around 7 because I have another plan.

Minjung: What do you have tomorrow at 7 p.m.?

Tim: I am planning to meet my classmates for our school project.

Minjung: Try to stay longer if you can. Jina is planning something special for her friends.

Tim: Okay. I will try to reschedule my plan for tomorrow.

Pair Activity

Practice each of the conversation again. Use your own stories or different ideas.

_____

_____

_____

_____

_____

_____

_____

_____

_____

_____

_____

_____

_____

Pointers to Remember

Native speakers often reduce the sound of 'going to' to 'gonna' and 'want to' to 'wanna'. Although the use of 'gonna' and 'wanna' is very common in spoken language, it is not recommended to use in writing. Also, the reduced form is used in an informal context, so in a formal setting, do not use 'gonna' or 'wanna'.

Class Activity

What is your future Plan? Ask the following questions to your classmates. Find out their plans.

Questions	Name	Extra Information
1. Will you graduate in _____?		
2. What are you planning to do this summer?		
3. What is your plan for the weekend?		
4. What will you have for dinner?		
5. Who will you marry?		
6. When will you buy a car?		
7. What are you going to do after you graduate?		
8. When are you planning to travel?		
9. What are you going to do this Friday night?		
10. Your own question.		

Grammar Practice

Future Tense: Future Events

We use the future tenses 'be going to' and 'will' to talk about future events. Use 'be going to' when the decision is planned and use 'will' when you want to make a promise or make a prediction for a future event. 'Going to' is often used for a planned decision while 'will' is used for a spontaneous decision.

> **Example:** I made plans for the summer. I am going to travel to New York.
>
> I am not sure of my plans for the weekend. I will probably visit my parents in Seoul.

Future time expressions can come at the beginning or at the end of the sentence. When it is at the beginning of the sentence, put a comma (,) after the time expression.

Next Friday	tomorrow morning	later tonight
Next day	tomorrow afternoon	later this afternoon
Next week	tomorrow evening	later this weekend
Next weekend	the day after tomorrow	soon
Next month	the day after next week	later
Next year	a week after today	later this afternoon
Next time	two days after today	later tonight

Comprehension Check Exercise

Create a calendar and fill in your schedule for next week, next month, or next year. What are your plans? Write important activities on your calendar. Share the information with your partner. Use the future tense verbs (going to & will) with future time expressions when sharing your schedule.

> **Example:** I am going to get a haircut tomorrow.

Tomorrow	Next Week	Next Month	Next Year

Pair Activity

What are your predictions for the year of 2030?

Where will you be in 2030? What will you be doing in 2030? How will the world be different in 2030? How will you be different in 2030? Think about the changes in yourself and of the world. Make interesting sentences about your predictions. Share your predictions with your partner.

> **Example:** I will have a nice job in 2030. In 2030, I will be _____ years old.

1. _____

2. _____

3. _____

4. _____

5. _____

6. _____

7. _____

8. _____

9. _____

10. _____

Class Activity

Where will your classmates be in 10 years? Find out by asking yes/no questions with will (will + base verb). Interview your classmates and share their answers to the class.

Example: Will you have a pet in 10 years?

Yes/No Questions	classmates	Extra Informations
1. ...have a spouse....?		
2. ...have a good job...?		
3. ...be working for an airline...?		
4. ...live in a foreign country...?		
5. ...speak English fluently...?		
6. ...make good money...?		
7. ...have a nice house...?		
8. ...love someone...?		
9. ...your own question...?		
10. ...your own question...?		

Photo by Chevanon Photography from Pexels

Key Expressions to Remember

1. **What are you going to do?**
   무엇을 할 겁니까?

2. **What is your plan for next week?**
   다음주에 대한 계획은 무엇입니까?

3. **What will you do?**
   무엇을 할 것인가요?

4. **Will you come to my party?**
   제 파티에 오시죠?

5. **I am going to visit New York.**
   저는 뉴욕을 방문할 예정입니다.

6. **I am planning to work in the summer.**
   저는 여름에 일할 계획입니다.

7. **It will probably rain tomorrow.**
   내일 비가 올 것입니다.

8. **I will buy a nice car.**
   저는 좋은 차를 살 것입니다.

9. **I am going to graduate in 2022.**
   저는 2022년에 졸업할 예정입니다.

10. **I have a meeting later this afternoon.**
    오늘 오후에 회의가 있습니다.

Airline Service Expressions

Immigration/Customs Check [입국 심사/세관 통과]

1. What is the nature/purpose of your visit?

방문 목적이 무엇인가요?

2. How long are you staying?

체류 기간이 어떻게 됩니까?

3. Where will you be staying?

숙소는 어디세요?

4. Can I see your passport and customs form, please?

여권과 세관 신고서 좀 보여주세요.

Courtesy of Pexel

5. May I have your nationality?

국적이 어디이십니까?

6. You still need to complete the customs form even if you have nothing to declare.

신고하실 물건이 없어도 세관 신고서는 작성하셔야 합니다.

7. Only one customs form is needed per family.

세관 신고서는 가족 당 한 장씩 쓰시면 됩니다.

8. Are you a US citizen or a resident?

미국 시민권자 또는 영주권자이십니까?

9. Do you have anything to declare?

신고하실 물건 있으십니까?

10. Are you carrying more than $10,000 dollars?

1만 달러 이상 소지하고 계신가요?

Practice Your English

A. <u>Writing Activity.</u> Use future time expressions to make statements about your-self or your family. Use 'be going to' to make complete sentences.

Next Friday	tomorrow morning	later tonight
Next day	tomorrow afternoon	later this afternoon
Next week	tomorrow evening	later this weekend
Next weekend	the day after tomorrow	soon
Next month	the day after next week	later
Next year	a week after today	later this afternoon
Next time	two days after today	later tonight

1. Later tonight, _____.

2. Next Friday, _____.

3. Tomorrow afternoon, _____.

4. Next month, _____.

5. Later this week, _____.

6. Next year, _____.

7. Tomorrow morning, _____.

8. At 3 p.m. today, _____.

9. This evening, _____.

10. The day after tomorrow, _____.

B. Speaking Activity. Use the following questions to ask your partner about his/her future travel plan.

1. Where are you going on vacation?

2. When will you go on vacation?

3. Who will you go with?

4. What are you going to do there?

5. How will you like it?

6. Which airline will you take?

7. Are you going to enjoy the trip?

8. Are you going to drive there?

9. Who will pay for the trip?

10. Will you stay in a fancy hotel?

Appendix 1   Unit Vocabulary

Unit 1

How do you do?	boarding pass
My pleasure meeting you.	proceed
informal greeting	aisle
formal greeting	complain
Welcome aboard.	final destination
traffic	packed
familiar	gesture

Unit 2

personal information	reservation number
collect	create
recently	moved
hometown	round trip
in charge of	one-way ticket
contact	flight
introduce	reservation number
hesitate	ground staff
campus	coworker
accept	confirm
responsible for	verify
load	conduct

Unit 3

current events	suitcase
plans	attach
commonalities	claim tags
running late	travel
neighborhood	visit
enjoy	season
baggage	sport
social event	scale

Unit 4

habits	healthy
routines	overeat
diligent	home cooked meal
fit	instant food
wonder	confusing
skip	breakfast
join	a window seat
nap	an aisle
seldom	preference
pre-assigned	offer discounts
workout	expressed

Unit 5

physical appearance	committed
mannerism	fellow classmates
emotion	previous

character trait	server
energetic	cooperatively
blond hair	unexpected situation
fingernails	talented
medium height	luggage
responsible	lounge

Unit 6

sightseeing	recommend
awesome	spend
skiing	upcoming
remain	souvenirs
relax	can't wait
art galleries	overhead bin
definitely	store
selected	consecutive

Unit 7

I don't share your point.	public transportation
roommate	meal options
country life	fond of
crowdy	adore
open space	seatback
celebrities	tray table
get away	live concerts
allow	recycle
citizens	run out of
prefer	passenger

Unit 8

instead	fancy
plain	workaholic
blind date	stressed
attractive	artist
high standards	earn
hire	borrow
consume	on board
famous	food items
competent	bright
similar	introverted

Unit 9

advice	junk food
loud music	issue
bother	neighbor
effective	craving
greasy food	gain weight
addicted	browsing
rarely	concerned
well-being	headache
blanket	medicine
allergies	tablet
cabin temperature	forgetful
deadline	piled
shopaholic	unnecessary item
charge on credit card	couch potato
cancel	worried

Unit 10

camping	cook outdoor meals
chilly	duty-free items
campfire	seat pocket
participate	allowance
paintings	exchange rate
memorable	currency
graduate	accept

Unit 11

bean sprouts	delicious
allergic	adventurous
degree	service industry
gain	confident
serve	abroad
surgery	award
discover	lottery
hunting	wallet

Unit 12

planned action	prediction
promise	promising
weather forecast	purpose
customs form	nationality
final destination	resident
carrying	reschedule
marry	spouse
relax	beach

Appendix 2   **Unit Key Expressions**

Appendix 2
Unit Key Expressions

Unit 1

1. How do you do? How are you? How are you doing? Hello. 안녕하세요.

2. How is it going? What is up? 어떻게 지내니? 잘 지내니?

3. How is everything? Is everything going OK? 잘 지내시죠?

4. Good morning/afternoon/evening. 좋은 아침(오후/저녁)입니다.

5. I am fine. Thank you for asking. How are you? 잘 지냅니다. 물어봐 줘서 고마워요. 잘 지내세요?

6. It is going fine. Pretty good. 잘 지냅니다. 잘 지내요.

7. It couldn't be better. 더 좋을 수 없지요.

8. I am busy as usual. 저는 항상 바빠요.

9. I can't complain. 불만은 없어요.

10. Nice/good to meet you. I am pleased to meet you. Pleased to meet you. 만나서 반가워. 만나서 반갑습니다.

Unit 2

1. Have you met, _____? This is _____. _____, 만나 보셨습니까? 이분은 _____이세요.

2. Let me introduce my friend, _____. 제 친구를 소개해 드릴게요.

3. I would like to introduce, _____. _____ 소개하고 싶습니다.

4. Please meet, _____. 여기 _____을 소개합니다.

5. There is someone I would like you to meet. This is _____. 소개하고 싶은 사람이 있습니다. 이분은 _____이세요.

6. It is a pleasure to meet you. My pleasure meeting you. 만나서 반갑습니다.

7. It is nice to meet you. 만나서 반갑습니다.

8. I have heard a lot about you. 말씀 많이 들었습니다.

9. I don't think we have met. 우리 아직 못 만나본 것 같아요.

10. So we finally meet. 마침내 이렇게 만나 뵙게 됐네요.

Unit 3

1. Today is a beautiful day. 오늘은 화창한 날입니다.

2. Do you have any plans for the weekend? 주말에 어떤 계획이 있나요?

3. Do you have the time? 몇 시인지 아시나요?

4. How is it going? 어떻게 잘 지내요?

5. I am doing great. 잘 지내고 있어요.

6. I am studying business. 사업을 공부하고 있습니다.

7. Are you enjoying this weather? 이 날씨를 즐기고 있습니까?

8. What are you studying? 어떤 공부를 하고 있어요?

9. What do you do? 당신의 직업은 무엇인가요?

10. I am a student. 저는 학생입니다.

Unit 4

1. What do you do in your free time? 여가 시간에는 무엇을 합니까?

2. What do you do for fun? 취미 생활이 뭐에요?

3. What is your hobby? 당신의 취미는 무엇입니까?

4. How often do you watch it? 얼마나 자주 시청하나요?

5. Do you exercise often? 자주 운동합니까?

6. Are you free this weekend? 이번 주말에 시간 있으세요?

7. I enjoy reading books. 저는 책을 읽는 것을 즐깁니다.

8. I usually meet friends on weekends. 저는 보통 주말에 친구들을 만나요.

9. I exercise twice a week. 저는 일주일에 두 번 운동을 합니다.

10. I am a flight attendant. 저는 승무원 입니다.

Unit 5

1. How would you describe yourself? 당신을 어떻게 표현 하시겠습니까?

2. How would your friends describe you? 당신의 친구들이 당신을 어떻게 표현 하시겠습니까?

3. What does he look like? 그는 어떻게 생겼나요?

4. How is her personality? 그녀의 성격은 어때요?

5. I believe I am a kind person. 저는 친절한 사람이라고 믿습니다.

6. My friends describe me as a positive person. 친구들은 저를 긍정적인 사람으로 묘사합니다.

7. I see myself as an outgoing person. 저는 제 자신을 사교적인 사람이라고 생각합니다.

8. She is tall and slim. 그녀는 키가 크고 날씬합니다.

9. He is muscular and attractive. 그는 근육질이고 매력적입니다.

10. She is understanding and compassionate. 그녀는 이해심과 배려심이 강합니다.

Unit 6

1. How was your summer vacation? 당신의 여름 방학은 어땠어요?

2. How was it? 어땠어요?

3. Do you have any plans for the winter? 겨울을 위한 계획이 있습니까?

4. Are you good at skiing? 스키 잘 타세요?

5. What did you do there? 거기서 뭐 했어요?

6. I did sightseeing. 관광을 했습니다.

7. I want to try camping. 저는 캠핑을 시도하고자 합니다.

8. I want to visit Paris. 저는 파리를 방문하고 싶습니다.

9. So did I. 저도 했습니다.

10. It was amazing. 그것은 훌륭했습니다.

Unit 7

1. Do you like watching movies? 영화 보는 걸 좋아합니까?

2. What do you think about live concerts? 라이브 콘서트에 대해 어떻게 생각하세요?

3. Do you agree? 동의합니까?

4. How do you feel about it? 이것에 대해 어떻게 생각하세요?

5. I understand your point. 당신의 관점을 이해합니다.

6. Sorry, but I think differently. 미안하지만, 저는 다르게 생각합니다.

7. I am afraid I don't agree with you. 죄송하지만, 저는 동의하지 않아요.

8. I am fond of meeting new people. 저는 새로운 사람들을 만나는 것을 좋아합니다.

9. We both enjoy camping. 우리는 캠핑을 즐깁니다.

10. I don't care for cold weather. 저는 추운 날씨를 좋아하지 않아요.

Unit 8

1. Do you prefer coffee or tea? 커피와 차 중 어떤 걸 드시겠어요?

2. Which do you prefer? 어느 쪽을 선호합니까?

3. What kind of tea do you like? 어떤 차의 종류를 좋아합니까?

4. What do you enjoy more, watching movies or reading books? 영화 보는 것과 독서 중 무엇을 더 좋아합니까?

5. What is important to you? 당신에게 중요한 것은 무엇입니까?

6. I prefer coffee. 저는 커피를 더 좋아합니다.

7. I like people who are kind. 저는 친절한 사람들을 좋아합니다.

8. I would rather have dinner. 차라리 저녁을 먹고 싶습니다.

9. I like dogs more than cats. 저는 개보다 고양이를 더 좋아합니다.

10. What else? 그 밖의 무엇을 드릴까요?

Unit 9

1. What is going on? 무슨 일입니까?

2. What should we have for lunch? 점심 식사를 무엇을 먹을까요?

3. How about soup and salad? 수프와 샐러드 어떻습니까?

4. What should I do? 제가 어떻게 해야 할까요?

5. I am worried about him. 그분이 걱정이 되요.

6. You have to eat healthy food. 건강에 좋은 음식을 먹어야 합니다.

7. You ought to eat more vegetables. 당신은 더 많은 채소를 먹어야 합니다.

8. You had better not eat fast food anymore. 더 이상 패스트푸드를 먹지 않는 것이 좋습니다.

9. You should not drink soda. 탄산 음료수를 마시지 않는 것이 좋습니다.

10. I eat too much junk food. 저는 너무 많은 정크 푸드를 먹어요.

Unit 10

1. How was your weekend? 주말 어떻게 보내셨어요?

2. What did you do there? 거기서 뭐 했어요?

3. How did you like it? 그거 어땠어요?

4. Did you enjoy the trip? 그 여행을 즐기셨어요?

5. We went camping. 우리는 캠핑을 갔다 왔어요.

6. I visited New York last year. 작년에 뉴욕을 방문했습니다.

7. We liked the trip. 우리는 그 여행을 좋아했어요.

8. I did not like the food. 저는 그 음식을 좋아하지 않았습니다.

9. I worked at a cafe. 저는 카페에서 일했습니다.

10. I studied music. 저는 음악을 공부했습니다.

Unit 11

1. What is your favorite food? 가장 좋아하는 음식은 무엇입니까?

2. Have you tried Indian food? 인도 음식을 먹어 본 적이 있습니까?

3. Have you worked there before? 전에 거기에서 일 해보셨나요?

4. Have you ever traveled abroad? 해외로 여행 한 적이 있습니까?

5. How long have you worked there? 그곳에서 일한 지 얼마나 되었습니까?

6. Where have you worked? 어디에서 일 해보셨나요?

7. No, I have never tried Indian food. 아니요, 저는 인도 음식을 한번도 시도한 적이 없어요.

8. I really enjoy the Korean food. 저는 한국 음식을 정말로 즐깁니다.

9. I want to try camping. 저는 캠핑을 가고 싶습니다.

10. So far so good. 지금까지 좋은 것 같아요.

Unit 12

1. What are you going to do? 무엇을 할 겁니까?

2. What is your plan for next week? 다음 주에 대한 계획은 무엇입니까?

3. What will you do? 무엇을 할 것인가요?

4. Will you come to my party? 제 파티에 오시죠?

5. I am going to visit New York. 저는 뉴욕을 방문할 예정입니다.

6. I am planning to work in the summer. 저는 여름에 일할 계획입니다.

7. It will probably rain tomorrow. 내일 비가 올 것입니다.

8. I will buy a nice car. 저는 좋은 차를 살 것입니다.

9. I am going to graduate in 2022. 저는 2022년에 졸업할 예정입니다.

10. I have a meeting later this afternoon. 오늘 오후에 회의가 있습니다.

Appendix 3   **Airline Service Expressions**

Unit **1** ···

Greeting Passengers [탑승 인사]

1. Good morning. Welcome aboard.
   안녕하십니까? 어서 오십시오.

2. Good afternoon/evening. It's nice to have you on board.
   안녕하십니까? 어서 오십시오.

3. May I see your boarding pass, please? Let me see your boarding pass. Will you show me your boarding pass?
   탑승권을 확인해 드리겠습니다. 탑승권을 볼 수 있을까요?

4. We have to recheck your boarding pass individually for security.
   보안을 위해 한 분씩 탑승권을 재확인하고 있습니다.

5. Thank you for your cooperation.
   협조해 주셔서 감사합니다.

6. Please proceed to the other aisle. Please proceed down this aisle.
   건너편 통로로 가시면 됩니다. 이쪽 통로로 가시면 됩니다.

At the Check-In Counter [체크인 카운터에서]

7. Where are you going today?
   어디까지 가십니까?

8. How many people are in your group?
   몇 분이십니까?

9. Where is your final destination for today?
   최종 목적지가 어디이십니까?

10. May I see your ticket and passport?
    여권과 항공권을 보여 주세요.

Unit 2

Ticketing at the Check-In Counter [일반 발권]

1. Do you have (a) reservation?

   예약은 하셨습니까?

2. Do you have any reservation number?

   예약번호는 가지고 계십니까?

3. Would you like to buy/purchase a ticket?

   항공권을 구입하십니까?

4. Would you like to go today? Where would you like to go?

   오늘 출발하십니까? 어디까지 가십니까?

5. Would you like to buy a one-way ticket or round-trip?

   항공권 구입은 편도이십니까? 아니시면 왕복이십니까?

6. Excuse me, could you show me your passport?

   실례합니다, 여권을 보여 주시겠습니까?

7. I would like to double-check your name with the passport.

   여권으로 이름을 다시 확인하고 싶습니다.

8. Could you please confirm the reservation?

   다시 한번 예약 확인 해 주시겠습니까?

9. How would like to pay? What would like to pay with?

   지불은 어떻게/무엇으로 하시겠습니까?

10. We accept a credit card, the Korean Won, the Japanese Yen, and the US dollar.

    신용 카드, 원화, 엔화, 미국 달러로 지불 가능합니다.

Unit 3

Baggage Check at the Check-In Counter [체크인 카운터에서 수하물 확인]

1. Do you have any baggage to check? Would you like to check in any luggage?

   맡기실 짐은 있으십니까?

2. How many bags/suitcases will you be checking in today?

오늘 맡기실 짐은 전부 몇 개이십니까?

3. Please put your baggage on the scale.

맡기실 짐은 여기로 올려 주시기 바랍니다.

4. Sorry, but could you put it one by one please.

죄송합니다만, 하나씩 올려 주시기 바랍니다.

5. Please have your baggage laid down on the belt.

짐은 벨트에 눕혀 주시겠습니까?

6. Whose bag is this?

이 짐은 어느 분 짐이십니까?

7. Mr./Mrs. _____, you have checked _____ baggage to _____.

_____손님, _____까지 짐 _____개를 부치셨습니다.

8. Please attach a name tag to your luggage.

손님 짐에 이름표를 달아 주시기 바랍니다.

9. Your baggage claim tags are attached to the back of the ticker here.

짐표는 항공권 뒷면에 붙여 두겠습니다.

10. Please keep the tags with you.

짐표를 잘 보관 하십시오.

Unit 4

Asking about Seating Arrangement at the Check-In Counter

[체크인 카운터에서의 좌석 배치에 관한 문의]

1. Do you have any preference for a certain seat?

원하시는 좌석은 있습니까?

2. Would you like a window seat or an aisle seat?

통로하고 창가 쪽 중 어느 쪽이 좋으십니까?

3. Would you like to sit together? Would you like to sit next to each other?

함께 나란히 앉으실 수 있는 좌석으로 괜찮으시겠습니까?

4. If you don't mind, how about an aisle seat in the back?

혹시 괜찮으시면 뒤쪽 통로 자리로 드리면 어떨까요?

5. Let me find it for you. Please wait for a moment.

찾아보겠습니다. 잠시만 기다려 주세요.

6. You have already pre-assigned to 33A, which is a window seat. Is this Ok for you?

현재 창가 쪽 자리인 33A로 사전 지정하셨는데, 그대로 드려도 괜찮겠습니까?

7. Today's seats are arranged 3-4-3 and which side would you prefer?

오늘 이 비행기 좌석 배치는 3-4-3으로 되어 있습니다만, 어느 쪽으로 하시겠습니까?

8. We ran out of seats that you can sit next to each other.

현재 나란히 같이 앉으실 수 있는 좌석은 없습니다.

9. How about sitting back and forth?

앞뒤로 나란한 좌석은 어떠신지요?

10. How about seats on the 1st floor?

1층 좌석은 어떠시겠습니까?

(Unit **5**) ⸳⸳

Visiting the VIP Lounge VIP [라운지 방문]

1. Welcome to _____'s VIP lounge.

_____ VIP 라운지에 오신 것을 환영합니다.

2. Would you show me your boarding pass?

탑승권을 보여 주시겠습니까?

3. You are free to enter the lounge.

라운지에 자유롭게 입장하셔도 좋습니다.

4. Do you have any membership card?

회원 카드가 있으십니까?

5. I am sorry but only one passenger can use this lounge.

죄송하지만, 손님 한 분만 이용 가능합니다.

6. We are very sorry, but you are not able to use the lounge.
   대단히 죄송하오나, 손님의 경우에는 라운지 사용이 불가합니다.

7. Would you please put your luggage in the coatroom?
   짐은 여기 COAT ROOM안에 넣어 주시겠습니까?

8. Could you take any valuable item with you?
   귀중품은 손님께서 직접 소지해 주시겠습니까?

9. You can use the computer in front of the desk anytime.
   안내 DESK앞 컴퓨터는 자유롭게 사용하실 수 있습니다.

10. Please enjoy the lounge. Do you have any questions?
    라운지를 즐기십시오. 질문 있으세요?

Unit 6

Securing Baggage [짐 보관 안내]

1. May I help you with your baggage?
   짐 보관을 도와 드릴까요?

2. This bin is full. Let me move your bag to another bin with more room.
   이쪽 선반은 가득 찼습니다. 가방을 더 많은 공간이 있는 다른 선반으로 옮겨 드리겠습니다.

3. Do you have any valuable item?
   혹시 귀중품은 없으십니까?

4. I'm sorry, but you cannot store your baggage here.
   죄송합니다만, 짐은 여기에 보관하실 수 없습니다.

5. We need to keep the aisle clear.
   통로에는 짐을 놓으실 수 없습니다.

6. Would you please store your baggage under the seat in front of you?
   짐은 앞좌석 아래에 놓아 주십시오.

7. We do not provide coat check service.
   의류 보관서비스가 제공되지 않습니다.

8. Would you please put your coat in the overhead bin?

의류 보관은 위쪽 선반에 보관해 주십시오.

9. You can store your baggage in this overhead bin.

이쪽 선반에 짐을 보관하실 수 있습니다.

10. Please check the baggage to our staff.

그 짐은 우리 직원에게 맡겨 주시기 바랍니다.

Unit 7

Meal Service [식사 서비스]

1. We will be serving lunch shortly.

곧 점심 식사를 제공 할 것입니다.

2. May I help you set up your tray table now?

지금 트레이 테이블을 세우도록 도와 드릴까요?

3. I'll ask the passenger in front of you.

앞좌석 손님께 협조를 부탁드리겠습니다.

4. Would you please return your seatback for the passenger behind you?

식사하시는 동안 뒤에 계신 손님의 식사를 위해 좌석등받이를 세워 주시겠습니까?

5. Would you like something to drink with your meal?

식사와 함께 음료는 무엇으로 드시겠습니까?

6. We have three meal options today: beef with potatoes, chicken with rice, and seafood with pasta.

세 가지 식사 옵션이 있습니다: 야채를 곁들인 소고기 요리, 밥과 닭고기 요리 그리고 파스타를 곁들이 해산물 요리.

7. I'm sorry. We have run out of beef. How about chicken, instead?

죄송합니다. 소고기는 모두 서비스되었습니다. 닭고기 요리는 어떠십니까?

8. Would you like some wine? We have white wine and red wine.

와인 드시겠습니까? 화이트 와인과 레드 와인이 있습니다.

9. Would you like some tea? We have green tea and earl grey tea.

차 드시겠습니까? 녹차와 얼그레이 차 있습니다.

10. Are you finished with your meal? May I take it?

식사 맛있게 드셨습니까? 치워드려도 되겠습니까?

Unit 8 ....

Snack Service in the Plane [스낵 서비스]

1. Would you care for a snack?

스낵 드시겠습니까?

2. We have chocolate chip cookies, pizza, and plain crackers.

스낵은 초콜릿 칩 쿠키, 피자, 일반 크래커가 있습니다.

3. Which one would you like?

무엇으로 드시겠습니까?

4. This is a hot pie. It has shrimp in it.

이것은 뜨거운 파이입니다. 안에 새우가 들어 있습니다.

5. I'm sorry, but personal food items are not allowed to consume on board.

죄송합니다만, 개인 휴대 음식은 기내에서 취식이 불가합니다.

6. We have spicy Korean instant noodles. Would you like to try?

한국 라면이 있습니다. 준비해 드릴까요?

7. Would you please wait for a moment?

잠시만 기다려 주시겠습니까?

8. It's hot, please be careful.

뜨겁습니다. 조심하십시오.

9. Would you like something to drink?

음료 한 잔 드시겠습니까?

10. Can I get you anything else?

더 필요한 것은 없으십니까?

Unit 9

Helping Sick Passengers [아픈 승객 안내]

1. Can I help you?
   무엇을 도와드릴까요?

2. Do you have any additional blanket?
   담요가 더 있습니까?

3. I'll check if there is any additional blanket.
   담요가 더 있는지 확인해 드리겠습니다.

4. I'll bring it for you right away.
   곧 가져다 드리겠습니다.

5. Excuse me, do you have anything for a headache?
   실례합니다, 두통약이 있습니까?

6. Yes, we have Tylenol on board.
   예, 기내에 타이레놀을 가지고 있습니다.

7. Do you have any allergies to any medicine?
   약 알레르기가 있습니까?

8. Would you like one or two tablets?
   하나 또는 두 개의 약을 드시겠습니까?

9. I will check the cabin temperature.
   기내 온도를 확인해 보겠습니다.

10. Would you like a hot drink?
    따뜻한 음료는 어떠십니까?

Unit 10

Selling Duty-Free Items [면세품]

1. We are selling duty-free items.
   면세품 판매하고 있습니다.

2. Would you like to buy any duty-free item?

면세품을 구매하시겠습니까?

3. Please see the in-flight catalog in front of your seat pocket.

좌석 주머니에 있는 잡지를 참고해 주십시오.

4. The duty-free allowance is three bottles.

면세기준은 술 세 병입니다.

5. How would you like to pay?

지불은 어떻게 하시겠습니까?

6. The exchange rate in the cabin is 1,170 won to the dollar.

기내 환율은 달러당 1,170원입니다.

7. Do you have any other currency, instead?

대신 다른 화폐는 없으십니까?

8. We take Korean Won, US Dollar, Japanese Yen and Chinese Yuan.

사용 가능한 화폐는 한국 원, 미국 달러, 일본 엔, 중국 위안화입니다.

9. You can pay by cash and credit card together.

카드와 현금을 같이 결제하실 수 있습니다.

10. We accept all major credit cards.

저희는 모든 주요 신용 카드를 받습니다.

Unit 11 ·······

Beverage Service [음료 서비스]

1. Would you like something to drink?

음료 한 잔 드릴까요?

2. Would you like ice with your drink?

얼음과 함께 드시겠습니까?

3. May I open your tray table?

테이블 열어드리겠습니다.

4. We offer juice, soft drink, wine, beer and so on.

주스, 탄산음료, 와인, 맥주 등이 제공되고 있습니다.

5. What kind of drink would you like?

어떤 음료로 드시겠습니까?

6. Here is your apple juice.

말씀하신 사과 주스입니다.

7. Which one would you like?

무엇으로 드시겠습니까?

8. Please enjoy your drink.

맛있게 드십시오.

9. Would you like some more tea?

홍차 더 드시겠습니까?

10. May I take your cup if you are finished?

다 드셨으면 컵을 치워드려도 되겠습니까?

(Unit **12**) ···

Immigration/Customs Check [입국 심사/세관 통과]

1. What is the nature/purpose of your visit?

방문 목적이 무엇인가요?

2. How long are you staying?

체류 기간이 어떻게 됩니까?

3. Where will you be staying?

숙소는 어디세요?

4. Can I see your passport and customs form, please?

여권과 세관 신고서 좀 보여주세요.

5. May I have your nationality?

국적이 어디이십니까?

6. You still need to complete the customs form even if you have nothing to declare.

신고하실 물건이 없어도 세관 신고서는 작성하셔야 합니다.

7. Only one customs form is needed per family.

세관 신고서는 가족당 한 장씩 쓰시면 됩니다.

8. Are you a US citizen or a resident?

미국 시민권자 또는 영주권자이십니까?

9. Do you have anything to declare?

신고하실 물건 있으십니까?

10. Are you carrying more than $10,000 dollars?

1만 달러 이상 소지하고 계신가요?

Appendix 4 — Irregular Verbs 불규칙 동사

Base Form	Past Simple	Past Participle
be (am,is,are)	was, were	been
become	became	become
begin	began	begun
bend	bent	bent
bet	bet	bet
bid	bid	bid
bite	bit	bitten
blow	blew	blown
break	broke	broken
bring	brought	brought
build	built	built
burn	burned or burnt	burned or burnt
buy	bought	bought
catch	caught	caught
choose	chose	chosen
come	came	come
cost	cost	cost
cut	cut	cut
dig	dug	dug
do	did	done
draw	drew	drawn
dream	dreamed or dreamt	dreamed or dreamt
drive	drove	driven
drink	drank	drunk
eat	ate	eaten
fall	fell	fallen
feel	felt	felt

Base Form	Past Simple	Past Participle
fight	fought	fought
find	found	found
fly	flew	flown
forget	forgot	forgotten
forgive	forgave	forgiven
freeze	froze	frozen
get	got	got (sometimes gotten)
give	gave	given
go	went	gone
grow	grew	grown
hang	hung	hung
have	had	had
hear	heard	heard
hide	hid	hidden
hit	hit	hit
hold	held	held
hurt	hurt	hurt
keep	kept	kept
know	knew	known
lay	laid	laid
lead	led	led
learn	learned or learnt	learned or learnt
leave	left	left
lend	lent	lent
let	let	let
lie	lay	lain
lose	lost	lost
make	made	made
mean	meant	meant
meet	met	met
pay	paid	paid

Base Form	Past Simple	Past Participle
put	put	put
read	read	read
ride	rode	ridden
ring	rang	rung
rise	rose	risen
run	ran	run
say	said	said
see	saw	seen
sell	sold	sold
send	sent	sent
show	showed	shown
shut	shut	shut
sing	sang	sung
sink	sank	sunk
sit	sat	sat
sleep	slept	slept
speak	spoke	spoken
spend	spent	spent
stand	stood	stood
swim	swam	swum
take	took	taken
teach	taught	taught
tell	told	told
think	thought	thought
throw	threw	thrown
understand	understood	understood
wake	woke	woken
wear	wore	worn
win	won	won
write	wrote	written

Appendix 5 — Answer Key 응답키

Unit 1

Warm Up Activity

1. Formal
2. Informal
3. Informal/Formal
4. Formal
5. Informal

Comprehension Check Exercise

1. B. Hey, Jane.
2. D. Good day, Madam.
3. A. How do you do?
4. C. I'm well, thank you. And you?
5. E. How are you, Ms. Lois?

Unit 2

Warm Up Activity

This is David Kim
He is from Busan.
He is 21 years old.
He is a student.

Comprehension Check Exercise

1. Hello, Dr. Ward. My pleasure meeting you. I am _____ from English department.
2. Hi, Ken. So nice to meet you. I am _____. I am from Korea.

3. How do you do, Ms. Park? My name is _____. Where are you from?

4. Hello, James. Welcome to our neighborhood.

5. How are you, Jenny? Welcome to _____ Air! Nice to meet you!

Unit 3

Warm Up Activity

1. What a nice day today! Are you enjoying this weather?

2. Did you watch the soccer game last night? I can't believe we won. I am so excited for the next game.

3. I am studying psychology. What are you studying?

4. Where did you get your jacket? It is really nice!

5. Do you have the time? The bus is late today.

Comprehension Check

1. A: I like your shoes. They are so pretty. Where did you buy them?

2. A: I believe the bus is running late this morning.

3. A: Did you watch the game last night?

4. A: What are your plans for the weekend?

5. A: Are you enjoying the weather?

Conversational Techniques

1. Asking questions:

   * What are you studying?

   * How about you? What is your profession?

2. Showing interest:

   * Really?

   * How interesting!

3. Agreeing:

   * It sure is.

4. Using echo question:

   * Are you?

5. Using echo word:

   * Hong Kong?

Unit 4

Warm Up Activity

1. A flight attendant provides in-flight service to airline passengers.

2. A nurse takes care of sick people.

3. Lawyers practice law.

4. Computer engineers build computer programs.

5. An actor plays a character in a movie.

6. Artists make art.

7. Air traffic controllers direct airplanes.

8. Wedding planners plan weddings for brides and grooms.

9. Bus drivers drive passengers to destinations.

10. A hotel receptionist help customers with reservations.

Comprehension Check Exercise

A.   1. always - all the time

2. almost always - many times

3. usually - generally

4. often - frequently

5. sometimes - once in a while

6. seldom - hardly ever

7. never - not at all

B.   1. usually

2. always/never

3. three times a week/always

4. always/in the afternoon

5. often/usually

6. every evening/always/never

Unit 5 ....

Warm Up Activity

1. C-energetic
2. C-smart
3. E-happy
4. M-nervous
5. C-talkative
6. M-good
7. P-gorgeous
8. P-thin/fit
9. P-blond
10. M-friendly

Comprehension Check Exercise

A. 1. tall
2. creative
3. bright
4. graceful
5. muscular
6. friendly
7. gorgeous
8. calm
9. active
10. shy

B. Are you creative?
Is your brother tall?
Is your friend gorgeous?
Are you calm during stressful situations?
Are you active at school?
Are you shy?

Is your sister friendly?

Are you always cheerful?

Unit 6 ··

Warm Up Activity (* Answers will vary.)

A. I went fishing this summer.

B. I went shopping in Paris two years ago.

C. I went sightseeing in Canada this summer.

D. I have never tried jet skiing.

E. I have never tried rock climbing.

F. I went bike riding when I visited Spain.

G. I went hiking last weekend.

H. I have tried scuba diving before.

I. I have never tried sailing.

J. I went camping two years ago.

K. I have tried kayaking before.

L. I have tried sun bathing before.

M. I have never tried bungee jumping.

O. I went skiing in Colorado last winter.

Comprehension Check Exercise

1. spent

2. used

3. plan

4. went

5. visit

6. took

7. met

8. stay

9. sent

10. buy

Unit 7

Warm Up Activity

1. Agreeing

2. Disagreeing

3. Disagreeing

4. Disagreeing

5. Agreeing

6. Agreeing

7. Agreeing

8. Disagreeing

9. Agreeing

10. Disagreeing

Comprehension Check Exercise

1. H for habits

2. G for general facts and truths

3. O for opinions and feelings

4. H for habits

5. G for general facts and truths

6. H for habits

7. H for habits

8. G for general facts and truths

Unit 8

Warm Up Activity (*Answers will vary.)

1. I prefer dogs.

2. I much prefer watching movies.

3. I like going to the live concert more than listening to music.

4. I prefer hamburgers.

5. I prefer drinking tea.

6. I much enjoy studying more than working.

7. I prefer relaxing.

8. I prefer the country.

9. I much enjoy sushi more than steak.

10. I like apples more than oranges.

Comprehension Check Exercise (*Answers will vary.*)

A. 1. I like people who are funny.

2. I ate dinner that was quite tasty.

3. My brother works for a company that makes cars.

4. She likes watching movies that are romantic.

5. I read a book that is interesting.

6. We need to hire someone who is bright.

7. He doesn't like eating food that is spicy.

8. I have a car that is reliable.

9. A great friend is someone who is loyal.

10. I prefer people who are kind.

B. 1. He is a successful person who works hard for his business.

2. I have a friend who speaks five languages.

3. I visited a beautiful city which was in France.

4. I read a book that was famous and old.

5. I borrowed a car that was fancy and expensive.

6. My boss is workaholic who is always stressed.

7. I am dating a person who lives in London.

8. I have been living in New York which is a great place for artists.

9. I met a person in San Francisco who works for a famous tech company.

10. They were successful students who earned academic scholarships throughout their college years.

Unit **9** ....

Warm Up Activity

1. should
2. should not
3. have to
4. don't have to
5. should

Comprehension Check Exercise A (*Answers will vary.)

1. You should first talk to your parents and discuss this matter with them. Then together come up with a plan to help your brother.
2. She should see a therapist. Or your family should take the phone away from her.
3. You should tell your friend that perhaps too much exercising is making him have joint pain.
4. You have to carry a small note with you all the time and write down important dates or events.
5. You should find a new roommate.
6. You should talk to your friend and tell her that you are really worried about her.

Comprehension Check Exercise B

1. had better take
2. should see
3. had better not drive
4. had better send
5. ought not to eat
6. ought to spend
7. Should/meet
8. shouldn't
9. had better
10. should avoid

Unit **10**

Warm Up Activity

1. present event

2. past event

3. present event

4. present event

5. past event

6. past event

7. past event

Comprehension Check Exercise A (*Answers will vary.)

1. was - I was sick yesterday.

2. went - My friend and I went shopping this weekend.

3. cooked - My mom cooked steak for dinner.

4. made - I made a pie before.

5. visited - I visited New York last year.

6. finished - I finished my homework.

7. turned - I turned 21 yesterday.

8. did not - I did not have breakfast this morning.

9. did - It did get cold.

10. could not - I couldn't come because I was sick.

Comprehension Check Exercise B

1. walked

2. slept

3. drove

4. wanted

5. liked

6. graduated

7. visited

8. worked

Unit 11

Warm Up Activity

1. I have ridden a horse.
2. My brother has worked in the engineering field.
3. My sister has traveled to France.
4. I have not worked at a cafe.
5. I have tried bungee jumping.

Comprehension Check Exercise A

1. Yes, she has.
2. She hasn't tried Pad Thai because she is allergic to peanuts.
3. Pad Thai is a Thai dish made with wide noodles, bean sprouts, onion, egg, and finely grounded peanuts.
4. The interviewee has worked in a family restaurant and a cafe.
5. The interviewee has worked for the marketing company for about a year.
6. No, she hasn't.
7. I think the interviewee is suitable for the cabin crew position.

Comprehension Check Exercise B

1. lost
2. has visited
3. have worked
4. have found
5. went
6. has known
7. has played
8. missed
9. finished
10. lived

Unit **12**

Warm Up Activity

1. prediction
2. planned action
3. prediction
4. prediction
5. planned action
6. planned action
7. prediction
8. prediction
9. prediction
10. prediction

Comprehension Check Exercise (*Answers will vary.)

* I am going to watch a movie tomorrow,
* I think it will rain tonight.
* I will finish my project next week.
* I am going to move to a new city next month.
* I will graduate next year.

Appendix 6   Grammar Index

References

Celce-Murcia, M. & Larsen-Freeman, D. (2015). *The Grammar Book: Form, Meaning, and Use for English Language Teachers* (3rd ed.). Heinle & Heinle Publishers.

Ciolli, C. (2018, January 29). *Beyond the Handshake: How People Greet Each Other Around the World.* Retrieved from https://www.afar.com

Lee, J. (2017). *English Interview for Cabin Crew: Mastering English Interviewing Skills.* Hanol Publishing Company.

Morton, C. (2018, September 25). *The 10 Most Popular Cities.* Retrieved from https://www.cntraveler.com

Robinson, L., Smith, M., Segal, R. (2019). *Stress Management: Using Self-Help Techniques for Dealing with Stress.* Retrieved from https://www.helpguide.org

Spillane, R. (n.d.). *Best in Flight Snacks, Ranked* [web log post]. Retrieved from https://spoonuniversity.com

Top 5 Duty Free Airports in the World. (2017, November 28). Retrieved from https://flyinganarchy.com/top-5-duty-free-airports-world

20 of The Weirdest Habits That Celebrities Have. (n.d.). Retrieved from https://www.lolwot.com

글로벌 영어

항공 서비스 토크가 있는 일상 영어 회화

초판 1쇄 인쇄   2019년 8월 5일
초판 1쇄 발행   2019년 8월 10일

저 자	이 선 규
펴낸이	임 순 재
펴낸곳	**(주)한올출판사**
등 록	제11-403호
주 소	서울시 마포구 모래내로 83(성산동 한올빌딩 3층)
전 화	(02) 376-4298(대표)
팩 스	(02) 302-8073
홈페이지	www.hanol.co.kr
e-메일	hanol@hanol.co.kr
ISBN	**979-11-5685-785-3**